The Language of Television

Uses and abuses

ALBERT HUNT

The Language of Television

Uses and abuses

With a Foreword by
Raymond Williams

Eyre Methuen · London

First published in Great Britain in 1981 in simultaneous
hardback and paperback by Eyre Methuen Ltd, 11 New Fetter
Lane, London EC4P 4EE

Typeset by Computacomp (UK) Ltd, Fort William, Scotland
Printed in Great Britain by
Redwood Burn Ltd,
Trowbridge & Esher

ISBN 0 413 33730 8 (Hardback)
      0 413 33740 5 (Paperback)

CONTENTS

ACKNOWLEDGEMENTS

I should like to express particular thanks to the following people, without whom this book would have been impossible:

Brian Groombridge, who advised the Independent Television Authority to give me the Fellowship which enabled me to begin work on the book.

The IBA (as it had now become) for having been so patient and tolerant while the book was being written.

Arthur Arnold, of Bradford College, who supervised the work.

Bradford College for having given us the use of their equipment.

Ken Sparne, for having provided the technical information, as well as helping to develop the work.

The Bradford school-leavers who helped to invent the video games, gave us material, and created *Spies at Work*.

The other members of the video team – Maurice Burgess, Rodney Challis, Carol Crowe, Paul Kerrigan, Keith Knowles, Larraine Hudson, Roger Simcox, Ian Taylor, Chris Vine.

Kathryn Perrill, for transcribing the video scripts.

Roberta Bonnin, for checking the proofs, and for her advice, encouragement, criticism and help with the writing.

And my family for their patience and help.

A.H.

FOREWORD

by Raymond Williams

There is now a great deal of writing about television, of various kinds. This book is different from any of them, and its originality is important.

Most writing about television is in the form of newspaper reviews of particular "programmes", as we call them. Yet actually what gets written about is not programmes but isolated shows, plays, presentations, discussions, documentaries. This follows from traditional newspaper reviews of books, plays and films. It can be useful if it is well done, and it has a certain interest however it is done, since television is one of the few interests we all now share in direct ways, and we obviously all want to talk about it or, for different reasons, to hear other people talking about it. In fact in one way this sort of writing is very unlike reviews of books, plays and films, which in most cases only the reviewers have yet seen, and which the rest of us read, in part, to get an idea of whether we want to see them. In television reviews, what is being written about is what we have already seen, and what quite often we shall have no chance to see again. So it relates, really, or ought to relate, to the process of talking over some common experience, and getting our ideas and feelings about it clear.

But this may be very difficult to do if only isolated programmes are written about, one after another, day by day and week by week. What can be missed is what is really involved in that word "programme". Programme came to be used as a general word for almost anything — a play, a documentary, a musical, a comedy show, a sports transmission, a discussion — because underlying all these was the fact of a *programme* in the original meaning – a plan of intended proceedings. What television offers is indeed this planned and announced sequence – or on different channels alternative sequences – of many kinds of production. And then for most of us the television experience, at its most central, has to do with these sequences of very diverse kinds of production. Of course we make our own selections within the available sequences, but many of us watch, even on a single evening, on the same screen, things as different as the news, a film, a discussion, an episode of a serial, a documentary, a play. Many of us now give more time to this watching than to something as important in our lives as preparing and eating food.

What has then to be thought and talked about, in these overlapping common experiences, is obviously more than the nature and quality of particular "programmes" – this or that specific production. It is this larger area that needs to be explored. There have been attempts to do this, in different ways. One way is that of general observational sociology, trying to answer such questions as whether violence on television affects actual social behaviour, or whether politics on television affects how we think and vote. This kind of study is useful, but it is not often very close to the material of television itself, in its actual processes. It is concerned with generalised content, and then, through its methods of questionnaire and survey, with generalised results. Thus on its own, even at its best, it can address itself to only parts of the common experience.

Some more recent work has moved closer. There have been detailed analyses of how particular productions are constructed, and what conventions they depend on. There have been analyses of the production of television news, by the *Bad News* group at Glasgow University, and of discussions and documentaries by writers associated with the periodical *Screen* and with the Centre for Contemporary Cultural Studies at Birmingham University. I have myself attempted some related work. When for some years I did a monthly television article for *The Listener* I tried to pull out certain kinds of television – sport, crime plays, interviews, advertising and so on – and say something more general about them. In my book *Television: Technology and Cultural Form* I tried to take this further and then to explore the ideas of sequence and "flow" – the succession and interrelation of different kinds of production, unified in certain ways by the television situation itself.

What Albert Hunt has now done is different from these kinds of work, though it is obviously related to them. His first part belongs to this development, and is given a particular edge by his idea of the "hidden curriculum" of television, and by his especially important distinction between the underlying assumptions in what can be classified, broadly, as entertainment and informational or educational productions. His remarks on the language and underlying relations of some popular television comedy are interesting in themselves and as they bear on the question of what we mean and should mean by "serious" television. His account of a divided world, in informational and educational work, is then the bridge to the second and most important part of his book.

What is original and striking about this second part is what can be learned, not from separated observation or analysis, but from the interaction of our ordinary experience of television and the practical experience of using video systems to make work on our own account. His detailed accounts of the various projects are fascinating in themselves, and for what they show us, by contrast, about the general television experience and the complex and often hidden society in which it occurs. These project reports will be of continuing interest to everyone seriously interested in television, but of course especially to teachers and to others directly concerned with the difficult and uncertain relations between television and our normal educational systems.

The broader aim of the book then comes into focus. Albert Hunt came to this work not only with particular interests and experiences in adult education, but with a broader and deeper interest in popular education as a whole. He is undoubtedly right in seeing that we have to include television in any current thinking about popular education, and in our thinking about the relations between popular education and the general structures and possibilities of modern societies. Because his interest is so much in activity and experiment, he has taken these central problems of our culture into an unusually open and active dimension. He has tackled not only the real links between television and popular education, but the inert, the conventional and often the false links, which have been put in place with so little public information and discussion. Thus a contemporary debate which is relatively familiar, in broad and often abstract terms, is given a liveliness and a specificity which should lead to many new practical arguments and experiments.

It would be good to think that in, say, five years time we might have hundreds of reports on comparable projects and experiments, thought through and analysed and discussed in an extending common activity. Whether we get them or not depends on many decisions and struggles in a much wider area of social and political life, but, at least, here, we see the kinds of work that can be done, their general educational and cultural relevance, and the active arguments, within and beyond the book, that they lead to.

INTRODUCTION

This book began its life as a report on a one-year project initiated by the Independent Television Authority (now the Independent Broadcasting Authority). The aim of the project was to explore ways of using the forms of television entertainment as instruments of adult education. Adult education as I defined it was "education for democracy" – an education that would help to enable people to understand, control and, where necessary, change their environment.

The project was planned in three stages.

The first stage would involve an attempt to examine, from the point of view of a regular TV watcher, the kind of education that popular television was tending to give, night by night, to the mass audience. I intended to approach this stage, not as a scientific researcher, but as a regular viewer myself. TV addicts (of whom I'm one) don't sit in front of the box with notebooks in hand. But they do swap stories of what they remember seeing. I planned to try and analyse, from my own nightly responses, precisely what television was tending to teach *me*.

The second stage would involve a closer analysis of a particular adult education series on Independent Television. The analysis would be followed by an attempt, using video, to make a programme offering an approach to the same subject built on entertainment forms. The series chosen was one intended to give parents information about what goes on in secondary schools – Granada's *Open Day*. Our alternative programme (made by the Media in Education Unit at Bradford College) was eventually called *Open Night*.

The third stage was planned as an experiment in using a

popular entertainment form to communicate information of some complexity. We eventually chose an episode in scientific history – Kepler's struggle to define the orbit of the planet Mars, as described by Koestler in *The Sleepwalkers* – and tried to present it in the form of one of those old movies that provide a staple diet of TV entertainment, *The Maltese Falcon*. A specific aim was to try and bridge the gap between what C. P. Snow once called "the Two Cultures".

The book consists very largely of an account of what was discovered in these three stages. But, while working on the project, and, later, while trying to write the report, I became increasingly aware of whole additional areas of social experience that needed to be taken into account in any thinking about how television might be transformed into an instrument of education for democracy.

For example, while working in Australia, and, for short periods, in Czechoslovakia and East Germany, I began to realise, in a new way, how essentially authoritarian and undemocratic the structure of our own television industry is. In Australia, I could watch old movies all through the night, if I chose to. Who, in Britain, decided that I shouldn't have that choice? In Bratislava and East Berlin, in the heart of what we take to be intolerably oppressive societies, I found that viewers could tune in to western television stations that offered them a view of reality in open conflict with the consensus values of the socialist states. Why, in democratic Britain, were we so *protected* from ideas that challenged our consensus? Why did we so easily accept the impossibility of picking up alternative messages? Why was our debate limited to the question of which authority was going to be awarded, by Government licence, the fourth channel? A Technical Advisory Committee, I read, had estimated in 1972 that it would cost £1,500 million to cable up the entire nation to a capacity of 24 channels. The Committee had advised that the cost was prohibitive, and the Government had accepted the advice. But why had the question of whether to spend that amount of money in that particular way not been presented to *us*, the community, for debate? The fact that viewers in Czechoslovakia and East Germany could pick up western television was, of course, an accident of geography. But the fact that our own television services were so limited wasn't an accident at all. It was the direct result of political decisions that reflected a particular social structure. It seemed to me important to examine the *use* of our video experiments in this particular social context.

Again, in the period following the one-year project, my other adult education work brought me into contact with people experiencing conditions of life which are not normally recognised as existing in our social welfare societies. In the inner city suburb of Redfern, in Sydney (where I was supposed to be working on Black Theatre), malnutrition amongst the Aboriginals was, according to a report quoted in the Melbourne *Age*, worse than in most Third World countries. The infant mortality rate of Aboriginals throughout Australia was the second highest in the world. If talk about "education for democracy" meant anything, it seemed to me that I was forced to ask myself what *use* our work on television entertainment might be to Aboriginals whose school education had left them without even such basic knowledge as how to go about getting the dole.

Back in Bradford, helping to produce a community newspaper in a housing estate described by a local councillor as the Third World of Bradford, I learned almost by accident that the twenty-four-year-old girl who was putting the paper together was bringing up four children (a fifth was in an institution, the father had left home) on a social security cheque of £13.04 a week, plus the meagre family allowances. Her whole life was spent in keeping herself and her children alive − and in having to cope with a social welfare bureaucracy which was trying to teach her "responsibility". Again, any concept of using television entertainment as an educational tool had, I felt, to be seen in relation to the needs of people living in environments such as the Canterbury Avenue estate.

It was in the context of an authoritarian television industry, working in a society that tolerates intolerable social injustice, that a section of our work not originally planned for began to assume major importance. While preparing for the making of *Open Night*, we had spent a good deal of time working with fifteen to sixteen-year-old school-leavers in Bradford. We'd invented and played video games with them, and had gone on to make video programmes. Not problem documentaries about their own situation, but entertainments, mock advertisements, collective cartoons, irreverent versions of *This Is Your Life*, and ultimately a spy film, set in Berlin, but shot in an old Bradford hotel.

While we were working with them on the video, we came to learn about ways in which *they* were oppressed. We learned, for example, of the school where fifteen-year-old boys were caned daily for not doing homework, or for getting answers wrong. We became aware of *their* awareness that education had failed them, and of their resigned acceptance of their own situation. They understood very clearly that, from the schools' point of view, the successful pupils were those, the privileged minority (19 per cent in Bradford in 1975), who would go on to reap the career, status and economic rewards of higher education. By the same token, they also understood that, from the schools' point of view, they were failures. (It didn't worry them overmuch: it simply meant that they'd decided, along with the great majority of the population, that education wasn't for them.)

In *this* context, the video images they'd created, which were eventually shown in the schools where they'd learnt to be failures, became tools for changing their relationships with the institutions that were oppressing them. They'd learned to handle equipment they'd never been allowed to touch before; they'd used that equipment to make programmes which entertained them and their friends, which grew out of the culture they were a part of, rather than the culture imposed by the school; they'd experienced the freedom to invent; and they'd been in control. Looking at what they'd made, alongside teachers and fellow-pupils, they experienced a sense of educational achievement, and also began to understand how the schools had, in fact, set limitations around them. The video had become an instrument for understanding and potential change.

The original ITA brief had been to explore possible relationships between entertainment forms on television and adult education programmes. But the work with the school-leavers demonstrated how the invention, through video, of entertainment forms could relate directly to enabling people to understand and cope with their environment. It seemed to me vital to describe and analyse this process, as a way of putting weapons into the hands of both teachers and pupils who might be working to transform their own institutions.

In the past few years, many schools, youth services and community centres have been equipped, often at considerable expense, with video systems. Often the systems have been seen as no more than teaching aids, technological devices for the passing on of received knowledge. And many of the community groups who have tried to use the hardware in the interests of social awareness have tended to imitate the dead forms thrown up by an authoritarian television industry.

Much of the work described in this book involves a search for new entertainment forms. But the search for new forms is seen throughout as a search for additional weapons of social and political change.

The work is offered in the hope that it may suggest yet another starting point, no more, for other people who are working to create urgently needed models of change.

PART ONE

The Television We've Got

exploring a hidden curriculum

In the past thirty years television has radically changed the way most of us spend much of our time.

The change came about very rapidly, sometime between 1950 and 1970.

In 1950 only ten per cent of the population of Britain had television sets. By 1963 only ten per cent were without them. The number of television licences issued rose from three million in 1953 to fifteen million in 1968. By the 1970's Raymond Williams was able to state "categorically" that "most people spend more time watching various kinds of drama than in preparing and eating food".

It's clear that any medium which engages so much of our time and attention must in some way be affecting our perceptions of the world. In other words, television is educating us already, whether we realise it or not.

What form does that education take? What view of the world and of our place in it is being offered, night after night, by the television we've got? And how would that view need to be modified if we were trying to invent new forms of television in order to create new forms of education?

The television we've got has, over the past thirty years, taught us three basic lessons, simply by becoming a part of the social landscape.

First, television has taught us to expect to have

professional entertainment on tap in our own homes. This expectation was unimaginable before the invention of radio, and it has led to the assumption of what is virtually a new human right: the right to be entertained in your own living-room. If the right is withdrawn — through a technicians' strike, or a black-out, or because the set breaks down — we feel physically deprived. The guardians of human rights talk a lot about freedom of speech and freedom of the press, but the right to express yourself in print only directly affects a small minority, the writers themselves. Whereas if the freedom to be entertained in your own home were suddenly suppressed, it would directly affect the entire population. Forced to choose between losing a couple of newspapers or a TV channel, most of us would, I suspect, give up the papers.

Secondly, television has taught us that we have another right — the right to choose *not* to be entertained. At its crudest, this right is expressed in the phrase, "You can always switch off." But it also includes the right to withdraw your attention, even if the set remains on, to vary your degree of concentration as and when you choose.

At first sight, this right may seem too obvious to be worth mentioning. But if we're thinking in terms of television's hidden curriculum, then it needs to be seen in relation to the hidden curriculum of schools. For in our compulsory education system the schools teach that the educator has the right to demand your full attention at any given time. In this context the right *not* to pay attention becomes an educational positive. (If a teacher bores you in school, you can't switch to another teacher. Conversely, a TV set never orders you to answer questions on what you've just seen.)

Thirdly, if television has taught us these rights, the television we've got has also taught us that the rights are only granted us by the grace of a higher authority which defines the limits within which they may be exercised. You may have the right to switch off, but you can't switch off what's not there. And what's there depends entirely on what "they", the higher authority, decide to allow.

In Britain, the highest authority is the Government. Over the decades successive Governments have decided that there should be first one, then two, and eventually three (sometime four ?) channels. Governments have also decided the terms on which these channels shall be licensed out. Companies which don't comply with these terms are simply prevented from broadcasting.

Television has taught us that this situation is entirely reasonable and normal. After years of regular viewing, it becomes difficult to believe that the three channels, in their present form, have not been there since the day of creation. Our imaginations may range over possible alternatives (a channel for pornography ?). Our direct experience, night after night, teaches us that *this* is what television must inevitably be.

And that it's unthinkable that the television services could function in any other way.

If television teaches us that the television we've got is the television that must be, it also teaches us that the terms on which that television is allowed to function are entirely reasonable and normal as well.

These terms are most clearly stated in the Independent Broadcasting Authority Act. The Act instructs the IBA to provide radio and television "as a public service for disseminating information, education and entertainment". The Authority is ordered to ensure that programmes "maintain a high general standard ... and a proper balance and wide range in their subject matter". Nothing must offend against good taste or decency, or "incite to crime or lead to disorder". A "sufficient amount of time" must be given to news, which must be presented with "due accuracy and impartiality". "Due impartiality" has also to be preserved "as respects matters of political or industrial controversy or relating to current public policy". The Chairman of the BBC's Governors accepted similar rules in 1964.

These terms have become so widely and unconsciously

accepted (if they were made the subject of a referendum, they would probably be universally affirmed), that it becomes difficult to recognise them as the reflection of a particular class ideology, with particular social and political interests. It also becomes difficult for us to recognise that they are in conflict with the way most of us want to *use* television.

The millions of people who bought or rented television sets in the late 1950's and early 1960's acquired them for one over-riding reason − they were hungry for entertainment. The commercial television companies, which began operating in the 1950's, held the promise of providing this entertainment: hence the sudden viewing explosion. The politicians, however, who laid down the terms on which the commercial companies would be allowed to operate, imposed on them the obligation to provide, not simply the entertainment that people were hungry for, but a "balanced" diet, which included information and education as well. Keith Waterhouse (novelist, playwright, and author of the highly popular TV comedy series, *Billy Liar*) wryly notes the results of this imposition in an article in the *Daily Mirror* of 8 June 1978: "Any ITV mogul will tell you − or perhaps he won't − that he didn't get where he is today by offering entertainment to the people. He had to pretend, with a straight face, that he was in the business of education. Look at the prospectuses of the commercial TV companies and you would think they were proposing a string of sixth form colleges … I'm reminded of the Victorians and their passion for 'improving literature'."

The reference to the Victorians is particularly apt. West Indian cricketer and historian, C. L. R. James, calls attention in his book, *Beyond a Boundary*, to a nineteenth-century popular hunger that closely parallels our contemporary hunger for TV entertainment − and he also notes authority's response to that hunger. "A glance at the world," he writes, "showed that when the common people were not at work, one thing they wanted was organised sports and games. They wanted them greedily, passionately.

So much so that the politicians who devoted themselves to the improvement of the condition of the people, the disciples of culture, the aesthetes, all deplored the expenditure of so much time, energy, attention and money on sports and games instead of on the higher things."

A glance at our world shows that when "the common people" are not at work, one thing they – we – want is television entertainment. But *our* politicians, devoting themselves to *our* improvement, have decreed that we can only have our entertainment as part of a "public service" which will also provide information and education. They've taught us that this state of affairs is normal and natural, but in fact the decree reflects a highly paternalistic and authoritarian view of "the masses", similar to that of the politicians of the late nineteenth century.

The nineteenth-century politicians, who were the representatives of the dominant middle-class ideology, saw the masses as a barbarous, irresponsible and potentially violent mob. G. A. N. Lowndes, in what is usually seen as the definitive history of public education in England in the late nineteenth century, quotes Dostoevsky's *Winter Notes on my Summer Impressions* on the population of London in 1863 : "For instance I was told that on Saturday night half a million working men and women with their children spread like a flood over the whole town ... Drunkenness is everywhere, but it is joyless, sad and gloomy ... The women are in no way behind, and get drunk along with their husbands while the children crawl and run about among them. Many of these husbands thrash their wives dreadfully. The children of these people, almost before they are grown up, go as a rule on the streets ... At the Haymarket, I observed mothers who brought their young daughters to trade with."

This was the kind of picture that Bradford MP Forster brought to his job as Vice-President in charge of the Education Department in the Gladstone government of 1868. In introducing his 1870 Education Act, Forster used the word "help". Of children between six and ten, he said, "we have helped about 700,000 more or less, but we have left unhelped 1,000,000, while of those between ten and twelve, we have helped 250,000, and left unhelped at least 500,000." Forster's way of "helping" the children of the working classes was to impose on them a compulsory education system which reflected the dominant middle-class values of discipline, competition, obedience to authority, and self-interest.

Our politicians follow those of the nineteenth century in seeing us as an irresponsible mass. Left to ourselves, we'd be a prey to the ITV moguls, who, in their greed for the quick profits made through advertising, would try and grab the largest possible audience by appealing to our most debased instincts and offering us an uninterrupted stream of rubbish, which, it's assumed, we would accept without question. To save us from ourselves, the politicians have forced the moguls to offer us dollops of "the higher things".

If we're trying to discover the hidden curriculum of the television we've got, it's necessary to ask what these "higher things" are saying to us. They are there as a result of decisions taken from a particular authoritarian point of view. How is this point of view reflected in the nightly offerings of information that the networks have been forced to include? What picture of the world, and of our place in it, is being communicated by these programmes which are, by decree, supposedly contributing to our improvement?

A glance at any evening's offerings, between six o'clock and bedtime, on either of the popular channels, reveals two distinct types of programme. There are, on the one hand, the programmes which do no more than try to entertain – during the period under review they ranged from the comparatively simple *Crossroads* and *Coronation Street* to highly sophisticated programmes such as *The Morecambe and Wise Show*, *The Two Ronnies*, *Till Death Do Us Part*, *Colombo* and *The Sweeney*. The entertainment programmes inevitably include a lot of situation comedies, a lot of action series, and a lot of old movies.

On the other hand, there are the offerings which are trying to tell us something – the *News*, *Panorama*, *World in Action*, *This Week*, *TV Eye*, *Tonight* (the names change from time to time, but the intention and the format remain the same). And there are the weekly documentaries.

The division between the two types of programme is clear and distinct, and teaches us a particular way of looking at the world.

First, the division teaches us that, in the words of Brecht, "there is a very sharp distinction between learning and amusing oneself." This in itself contains two hidden assumptions: that learning is essentially unentertaining, and that entertainment teaches us nothing.

Secondly, we're made aware of two different tones of address. The entertainment programmes normally address us in the manner of one adult talking to another: they invite us to share the world they create, and if we don't like that world, we simply move on.

The information programmes, on the other hand, address us as people who need to be told something. The language they use isn't the language we'd normally use in talking to each other. It's the language of what the film-maker, Luis Buñuel, once called "official reality". It's also the language we once grew accustomed to in the classroom, the language of those who are in the know, and whose job it is to pass the knowledge down to us. The newsreaders, the presenters of current affairs programmes, the expert interviewers who, night by night, interpret the world for us, are all like very affable schoolteachers. Like naughty schoolboys, we try to catch a glimpse of Angela Rippon's legs under the desk.

Thirdly, because of the clear distinction between information that we ought to know, and "mere" entertainment, we're made to feel that only the informing, authoritative tone is "serious". We're taught to equate knowledge of the world with the presence and language of expert authority. And so we see the world through authority's eyes, are conditioned to articulate what we see in authority's phraseology.

Finally, we're also assured repeatedly that the information we're receiving is "impartial" and "accurate". And so the sense of "impartiality" becomes associated with a particular tone. The tone is that of authority. When we're made to look at the world through authority's eyes, we're being encouraged to believe unquestioningly that we're seeing a picture of objective reality, which becomes identified with the "official reality" of authority. And since this is the *only* way news is presented to us, it becomes difficult to imagine that any other way of looking at the world could possibly exist.

What is this picture of the world that our television information services unconsciously equate with objective reality? (I stress unconsciously because the reason that the view is communicated with such conviction is that the communicators themselves aren't aware that they're expressing a view at all. They accept totally that theirs is the only objective way of looking at the world.)

The Glasgow University research unit which produced the book *Bad News* tried to construct the picture by recording every item of news televised over a long period, and analysing the results. They measured footage, examined the choice of visuals, studied the words, and reached the conclusion that what they called the "agenda" of the news programmes was both limited and biased.

Regular viewers, however, don't normally record and analyse programmes. All they're left with at the end of an evening is impressions – picked up alongside other, sometimes more vivid, impressions left by the entertainment programmes.

Two experiments we carried out at Bradford suggest that these impressions may be much more hazy than the makers of news and current affairs programmes would care to imagine. The makers are very conscious of their responsibility. They've been given the job of telling the "truth", without allowing their own personal bias to show. And they believe that if they fall short of what they regard as their standards of accuracy, they might do social harm by leading viewers in wrong directions. Our Bradford experiments could relieve them of some of their anxieties.

In the first experiment, a group of us looked carefully at a twenty-five minute news programme. Afterwards, each of us in turn, and separately, recorded on video a verbal description of what we thought we'd seen. We then looked at the recordings together. No two accounts agreed: every one of us had forgotten at least one significant item of news, and some of us had left out major stories. Yet we'd watched the programme, not as we would have watched it at home, sandwiched between other programmes, and with other things going on in the living-room. We'd watched it with concentration, as an isolated piece of television, knowing that we were going to have to describe what we'd seen. And we remembered as much or as little as we would have taken away from a formal lesson at school.

In the second experiment, we showed a recording of the *Panorama* programme about Solzhenitsyn to a group of students withoug telling them why they were seeing it. Afterwards, another group of students, who hadn't seen the programme, interviewed those who had, one at a time, on video. Several of those who'd seen the film couldn't remember Solzhenitsyn's name — some writer from Russia had landed somewhere in an aeroplane and had talked about his writing and about how bad Russia was. Others described things that weren't in the film at all, and that they'd clearly heard about Solzhenitsyn from other sources. One girl, a very bright design student, could only remember that there had been a man wearing a check jacket, and that at one point there had been some interesting ornaments behind him while he talked. Once again, the students had seen the film in conditions very different from those of the regular viewer at home.

The experiments suggest that in a normal evening's viewing only a fraction of the actual information that's offered is likely to stick, but that particular images might remain to build up a generalised impression. Clearly the images are more likely to be remembered if they're familiar through repetition. The images that we see most often are those of the newsreaders and the regular current affairs experts. In one way they *become* the news. The attitudes they present, night after night, are much more likely to affect our somewhat hazy grasp of the situation than any detailed account they give of the rights and wrongs of a particular issue.

What kind of general impression of the world remains at the end of a typical night's viewing? Remains, for example, on *me*, as a regular viewer?

I quote from some notes I made, at random, after one Monday night's viewing in March 1977. I hadn't intended to take particular notice of the news and current affairs programmes that night: but the next day, on impulse, I wrote down what I remembered. I didn't try to check what I thought I remembered against the official transcripts — regular viewers can't, and have to depend on their impressions.

The notes read as follows:

Last night I watched, in between other programmes, two BBC news bulletins, half an ITN news, two thirds of a *Panorama*, and a half of *Tonight*. During the evening, I also watched *Opportunity Knocks*; *Oh, No, It's Selwyn Froggitt*, which was responsible for my missing a third of *Panorama*; a mediocre Monday night film; and highlights from the Test Match.

On the first BBC news there were bombs and fires in Ulster. Later, a report came that an English businessman had been shot in his car. The Belfast business community said that the wave of bombings confirmed a Provisional IRA campaign against business. The BBC news included a long item about whether or not the "murder" of an 18-year-old member of the Royal Ulster Constabulary had been caused by an item in a BBC *Tonight* programme. Someone connected with the RUC said it had. A BBC official said it hadn't. He said he was sorry that a programme about the alleged ill-treatment of arrested people by the RUC should have been given this degree of importance. On the ITN news, the same RUC spokesman said that the RUC were reaching the point where they objected to being used as front-line troops.

BBC news also announced that the new Foreign Secretary was going to visit South Africa. He would be willing, said Angela Rippon, to meet Mr. Smith, as long as Mr. Smith would also go to South Africa. The Foreign Secretary would *not*, Angela Rippon stressed, be visiting Rhodesia.

The BBC cameras then visited Rhodesia. They went to a farm on which a European woman had been "murdered" by "terrorists". Her husband had died from a heart attack while shooting at the assailants. The daughter and son-in-law of the couple were interviewed. What particularly shocked them was that the attackers had had inside help — we were shown a lock that had been opened by one of the black house-boys. Why, the girl kept asking, should anybody have *wanted* to kill her parents? Her father had even resisted the idea of carrying a weapon. Nobody would ever attack him, he'd said, after all he'd done for these people. This was a beautiful country, the young people said. There was room here for everybody. There was room for millions of people.

Panorama was about India. I picked it up at a point where a BBC reporter was interviewing villagers for first-hand stories, relayed through an interpreter, about the excesses of forced sterilisation. A boy was asked if he'd been promised anything. Yes, he said, land and a house. Had he received anything? No.

Later, David Dimbleby interviewed Mrs. Gandhi. Why had she declared a state of emergency? She said that she'd had to interfere with the freedom of a few people who were threatening the stability of India. What freedom, she asked, did the masses of India have against their landlords and their employers? What freedom was there in poverty? Freedom, she said, would come from stability, economic growth. Dimbleby said he had first-hand accounts of the excesses of the sterilisation campaign. All excesses, she said, were being looked into. Why, Dimbleby asked, had she brought her son into the Government? Not the Government, she said: the Youth Congress. But hadn't he, Dimbleby, seen a calendar with a picture of her and her son together? Didn't this kind of thing damage her image? Mrs. Gandhi said she discouraged the building of images around herself. If she lost the forthcoming election, Dimbleby said, in what way did she think she would be to blame for her defeat? She wasn't interested, she said, in praise or blame. As long as she was in charge, she was responsible for the stability of India. She would go on working for that stability.

Back in the studio an announcer said that whatever she thought about praise or blame, the people of India would be showing whether or not they blamed her in the coming elections.

In *Tonight*, Ludovic Kennedy interviewed the Prime Minister of Singapore, Lee Kuan Yew. Kennedy asked Lee about press censorship. To which section of the press, asked Lee, was Kennedy referring? He presumed that Kennedy spoke Chinese, Malay, Tamil. He himself, he modestly admitted, spoke only three of the island's four languages: he had no Tamil.

Kennedy asked about political prisoners. Lee said he knew more about them than Kennedy: he'd fought alongside them against British colonialism. Did Lee, asked Kennedy, stick to a statement about freedom to publish he'd made 18 years ago? Lee admitted, with a smile, that possibly he'd mellowed since then. But weren't there, Kennedy insisted, political prisoners who'd been held in captivity for 13 years? There were three, said Lee. They were communists who believed in using both the ballot and the bullet. If they would renounce the use of the bullet they could be released tomorrow. Was Lee, then asking them to sign a paper? If they refused, would they be held indefinitely? There was no paper, said Lee. All they had to do was *say* they'd renounce the bullet. But, of course, they wouldn't, because they *believed* in violence. They saw themselves as Lenins and Maos. If the communists won, they'd be up there on the podium. They knew the rules, he implied. They were trying to overthrow him: he had to stop them. They knew why they were going to stay in prison.

Towards the end of the interview, Kennedy asked Lee why his picture wasn't everywhere, like the pictures of most dictators. Was he trying to avoid the glare of publicity? Lee looked towards the battery of cameras and lights, and smiled. Back in the studio the *Tonight* announcer also smiled. These oriental dictators, his manner suggested, whatever will they say next?

I've quoted the notes in some detail because the items described add up to a classic example of the kind of world picture our television services offer, without variation, night after night. (All the items happen to come from BBC programmes: but the difference between BBC News and ITN on any given night is marginal.)

In that picture, Britain is assumed to be the guardian of liberal, civilised values, which are being threatened by forces of irrational violence. (Sometimes the forces of irrational violence erupt in our own society, in the shape of strikes, accompanied by picketing. The picketing is always the result of "militants", who stubbornly refuse to listen to reason.)

The item about Northern Ireland is typical of the way our television services have been handling a war that's been going on for years in a region of the United Kingdom. The war in Northern Ireland has caught the television services in irreconcilable contradictions. On the one hand they're required to present the news with "impartiality"; on the other hand they're instructed not to "incite to disorder".

To present the news from Northern Ireland impartially would involve presenting the case for the Provisional IRA as fairly and accurately as possible. This would mean explaining the political rationale behind IRA actions. But to present the IRA case would be to provide arguments for the supporters of the IRA, which would be tantamount to "inciting to disorder". The television authorities avoid the problem by not presenting Northern Ireland as a political issue at all, but simply as a question of security: a *This Week* reporter, Peter Taylor, is quoted in the *National Times* of Australia (week ending 2 September 1978) as saying: "That's when you've got trouble. When you report on the Irish-British context and start examining British Government policy in Northern Ireland, as against examining the security problem."

In the absence of a political context, IRA actions emerge — as on this particular night — as expressions of a meaningless violence. Stores have been bombed. The Belfast business community says the IRA has launched a campaign against business. Nobody bothers to ask why. What's more, an *English* businessman has been shot. (IRA killings, particularly of people from the mainland, provide the main theme of our television's treatment of Northern Ireland: Northern Ireland makes the biggest news when IRA bombs explode in England.)

Television presentation of Northern Ireland persistently ignores the *political* viewpoint of one of the main parties of the dispute, and so we're given a highly partial view of the conflict. But this highly partial view is then offered in the language of "impartiality".

Occasionally, the "impartiality" is proved by the appearance of Provos on the screen. We've already been taught, night after night, to regard them as mindless thugs: we listen to such of their arguments as they're allowed to present with hostility and disbelief. The hidden curriculum has told us how we should see them — it takes an act of conscious will to look at them in any other way.

On other occasions, the "impartiality" is proved by references to the "alleged" misdemeanours of the security forces. The item on *Tonight*, about the Royal Ulster Constabulary's treatment of arrested people (referred to at length in the BBC News) comes into this category. In the news item, the BBC is shown to be a very serious, responsible body. They had to investigate the allegations against the RUC, in the interests of truth. And now an 18-year-old member of the RUC has been shot, and the RUC says the BBC is to blame. So the BBC will prove its commitment to truth – to "impartiality" – by investigating the allegations against itself.

The "impartiality" operates within a totally partial framework. The rightness of the British Army's presence in Northern Ireland is accepted without question. And so, too, is the inevitability of internment (in sharp contrast to Lee Kuan Yew's imprisonment of his political opponents, which is seen by Ludovic Kennedy as an act of political will by an unscrupulous dictator.) There's no criticism of the internment policy itself – only of "excesses" within that policy. And the "excesses" are, of course, "alleged" – even though Britain's treatment of prisoners in Northern Ireland has been condemned by an international court. An RUC spokesman will be there to deny them, or describe reports as "exaggerated". His presence will offer one more proof that the BBC is maintaining "balance" and "impartiality", even in news stories about itself.

The suggestion that a BBC news story may have been responsible for the shooting of a member of the RUC is clearly absurd (the IRA don't need the BBC to tell them that the RUC mistreat prisoners). But its effect is to reinforce the arguments used by both BBC and IBA to justify direct censorship of Northern Ireland news, usually described as "special treatment". (The IBA says "special treatment" is necessary because reports of violence in Northern Ireland are shown in Northern Ireland and "might encourage or excuse further killings or violence" – once again implying that the reasons behind the killing are largely frivolous and unconnected with a social reality that exists, whether reported or not.)

The conscience-searching, however, ("can it be that in our determination to be 'impartial' we've incited to disorder?") has the effect of leaving viewers with the impression that the BBC is a massively responsible institution, desperately trying to be fair to all sides, in an intolerably difficult situation. And of confirming the general impression that the war in Northern Ireland has little or nothing to do with political solutions.

The items dealing with Rhodesia demonstrate how the Rhodesian crisis had caught our TV services in a dilemma. On the one hand, as decent white liberals, we all knew that Ian Smith hadn't played the game: what's more, his unilateral declaration of independence hadn't been legal. So, in this news bulletin, Angela Rippon can safely express our approval that the Foreign Secretary won't go to Rhodesia to visit the bounder. On the other hand, throughout the crisis, TV assumed that we would never be able to resist a shudder when we heard of whites killed by blacks. Here, the shudder is aroused by the vivid report of the attack on a white farm.

The announcement of the Foreign Secretary's decision not to visit Rhodesia comes across on a very classroomy level – teacher is telling us something we ought to know, in a way that also tells us we ought to approve. But the film of the young people whose parents have just been "murdered" on the farm works in a very different way.

We're suddenly confronted, in the most direct possible manner, with human emotion. These two young people have just suffered in a shocking way. We see them there, still dazed and grief-stricken, but putting on a brave face. They're clearly nice, ordinary young people who wouldn't hurt anyone. We can't believe their parents would hurt anyone either. Yet they've been killed. As in the case of

Northern Ireland, we're faced with meaningless violence.

The sequence works in terms of tragic drama. We're invited to identify with the characters, to share their suffering. But in sharing their suffering, we're also being invited to identify with their view of the world.

Their view of the world is very simple. White people have made their homes in Africa. In doing so, they've "helped" the native population (as the Forster Education Act "helped" working-class children). They've "helped" them to such an extent that it becomes inconceivable that the natives should want to kill them. There could be room for everybody if only the natives would be reasonable. (The "everybody", of course, includes the white settlers who forcibly took the land in the first place.)

The view is that of a nineteenth-century British imperialism which saw itself as wholly liberal. But because it's presented in such a personalised way, it becomes hard to recognise as a political view at all. Politics is about the Foreign Secretary and Ian Smith, not about these young people, who therefore become victims of mindless savagery. Moreover, as viewers, we're put in the situation where the act of questioning this view of the world involves a kind of heartlessness. To make critical judgements about people who have suffered this kind of loss is to display a cruel lack of feeling.

It would be unreasonable to expect television news to set every human interest story in a detailed and reasoned political context. But by ignoring the underlying issues in this case, the BBC is, in effect, playing a political role. By the way our feelings are manipulated, we're encouraged to identify ourselves *with* the political aspirations of the white settlers (to hang on to their land) and, therefore, *against* the political aspirations of the black guerillas. Moreover, the imagery in which that invitation is cloaked evokes a traditional mythology of black treachery and white devotion to duty. The lock, opened from the inside, becomes a symbol of black betrayal: while the image of the father, fighting for his homestead while dying of a heart attack, is reminiscent of the world of nineteenth-century romantic fiction, in which brave white pioneers lost their lives defending conquered corners of civilisation against mobs of native savages.

What makes the mythology important is that it re-appears in our media whenever there are black/white confrontations in the news.

Compare the emotions stirred by the television images with those aroused by the *Daily Mail* at the time of the Stanleyville "massacre" in November 1962. The *Daily Mail* contrasted a Dr. Carlson, who met his "private Calvary" while serving "those who could not help themselves", with a "deaf mute called Kasango", who, "renowned for his brutality, is able to converse only in grunts and squeaks". The *Daily Mail* went on:

> He whined with rage as the guns of the Belgian paratroopers were heard on the outskirts of the city. Then the huge and loutish rebel gestured violently at his soldiers to begin the massacre. He himself emptied the magazine of his automatic rifle into the nearest white woman.

As Conor Cruse O'Brien pointed out in the *Observer* at the time of the Stanleyville incident, "Africans would like to be able to send paratroops to Dixie and South Africa to rescue Negroes from their brutal white guards." Such a concept, however, is outside the mythology. As good liberals we're assumed to believe that all human beings are equal. To the media, however, some are more equal than others. At the time of Stanleyville, the *Sunday Times* described the "systematic extermination" of 7,000 blacks as "almost overshadowing" the deaths of 130 white hostages. In the same way, the death of a white farmer, or of Elim Pentecostal missionaries (who later turn out not to have been killed by guerillas at all), makes television news. Whereas the day to day violence perpetrated by Ian Smith's regime against the black population isn't newsworthy at all.

From time to time, of course, there *are* programmes about the oppression of blacks in Rhodesia and South Africa. They're invariably presented by the resident experts. They make it clear that it's O.K. for all decent people to be against the regimes in Rhodesia and South Africa. They also confirm that "truth" is synonymous with the way David Dimbleby, Ludovic Kennedy and Robin Day interpret the world.

The *Panorama* and *Tonight* interviews, with Mrs. Gandhi and Lee Kuan Yew respectively, offer good examples of how the experts interpret the world.

The fact that the experts are resident is central. The regular viewer recognises them as permanent characters in the nightly soap-opera of current affairs, as familiar as Ena Sharples of *Coronation Street*. Their presence tells us that we can only hope to understand the world if we're as clever and informed as they are. In contrast, the people they're interviewing become the bit players. They may be at the centre of world events, but they're not at the centre of the current affairs programmes. We're only allowed to see of them as much as the experts allow to be revealed.

Mrs. Gandhi is faced with the overwhelming problems of a sub-continent that's suffering from an almost inconceivable population explosion. She's concerned above all about the stability of India. David Dimbleby could have questioned her about her concerns – *how* did she propose to liberate the masses from their landlords and their employers, and from their poverty? *How* could she stimulate growth? Instead, David Dimbleby asks her about her picture on a calendar, her image, and her inner feelings – how far does she *blame* herself. We're made to feel that Mrs. Gandhi hasn't quite lived up to the British notion of Fair Play, which is why she can be expected to feel a little guilt.

Lee Kuan Yew also isn't playing fair. Kennedy, like Dimbleby, pursues questions about censorship, the freedom of the press, the imprisonment of political opponents. And he, too, is interested in a picture – Lee Kuan Yew's portrait, which, suspiciously, is *not* on display.

What is striking is the smugness of the questions. Both Mrs. Gandhi and Lee Kuan Yew are aware that, when British interests were resisted in India and in Singapore, states of emergency were declared, the press censored, political opponents put in prison (the pattern is being repeated in Northern Ireland). They must find it difficult to take seriously the self-righteousness of the interviewers.

The interviewers, however, communicate to us, the viewers, by their self-assurance and their manner, that theirs is the only commonsense, reasonable, *unbiased* way of looking at the world – indeed, the only way of looking that it's possible to imagine. It happens to be the way of looking of the British middle-class.

The picture of the world that emerges from all four items is, in fact, remarkably consistent. The world is seen as a place to which Britain has exported a way of life. The way of life is based on decency, tolerance, fair play, a regard for personal liberty and for the freedom of the press. Britain's role has been that of her army in Northern Ireland – to keep the peace.

But there are people in the world who don't play the game. They kill, mindlessly, for no reason at all, in Northern Ireland and Rhodesia. They carry out social policies, such as forced sterilisation (the Indian version of compulsory education?), that demonstrate the tyrannous nature of their politicians. They censor news and put their political opponents in prison. They threaten the lives and property of decent Britons who never did anybody any harm.

Readers must judge for themselves how far the programmes I've analysed are typical, and how far the analysis is fair. The problem is that television's "official" view of the world is so all-pervasive that it is difficult even to formulate critical questions: the formulation itself demands a positive act of the imagination, the setting-up of an alternative vantage point, such as Marx set up in the nineteenth century (Marx offered, primarily, a *different* way of looking).

As I write, our television authorities are trying to report a lorry-drivers' strike. The strike is being reported, not in terms of a dispute between workers and employers, but in terms of how effectively the "responsible" trade union leaders can control the "militant" pickets. Within the partial framework, of course, impartiality is once again maintained – the pickets are invited to explain why they are behaving so unreasonably. When the "militants" point out that the strike could be ended if the employers would negotiate an agreement, they're accused of evading the question.

What the question should be is decided by the expert interpreters of "official reality".

"Official reality" is so all-pervasive on our screens that when a programme unexpectedly fractures the picture, the result is disturbing. When Mohammed Ali used his physical power to take over Michael Parkinson's chat show, in December 1974, and deliver a long, black-Muslim denunciation of "white devils", emphasising his points by stabbing with his huge finger at a book belonging to Parkinson, the conventions of the show collapsed. Parkinson sat slumped in his chair and the studio audience shifted uncomfortably. When, after Ali had run out of steam, a British boxer pointed out that there were black boxers in the English amateur team, and suggested that Ali should be working for integration, the audience applauded in relief – we were back on safe ground. But Ali growled, "Thirty-seven blacks killed in Chicago last weekend", and forced on us a view of reality radically different from the one our television normally takes for granted.

Usually, however, any variations from the official version are smothered in blandness. So, on a BBC-2 news programme (20 June 1978) a banker is interviewed about inflation. Given the fact that higher wages lead to inflation, he's asked, what does he think will happen in the next round of pay claims?

The banker says he doesn't think higher wages lead to inflation. He thinks it works the other way round. The interviewer is going on automatically to the next question, when he realises what the banker has said, and does what amounts to a double-take. He knows it's slightly off the subject, he says, but what the banker has said is very surprising. Will the banker please explain what he means? The banker talks monetary theory, incomprehensible to a layman. But the interviewer seems to be satisfied. He returns to the script: "In view of the increases in wages, what do you see happening?" Official reality, which affirms that higher wages are the main cause of inflation, has been re-imposed. But just for a moment it's been possible to imagine an alternative reality, a normality which might include the question, "Given the fact that inflation leads to demands for higher wages, what do you think should be done about industrialists who put up their prices?"

The concept of normality is at the centre of television's hidden curriculum. From time to time a mildly radical programme or series is presented – a re-appraisal, from a safe distance of time, of episodes in Britain's imperial past, an exposure of an isolated social abuse, aimed at stirring the public conscience. The presentations are labelled "controversial", so that we can be aware that we're being faced with something unusual. In the same way, the access series, such as *Open Door*, are, by definition, ghettos where minorities, whose voices wouldn't otherwise be heard, are given a slot to express their unorthodox opinions. Their ways of looking clearly *aren't* "normal", or they wouldn't be in that slot in the first place. Since they're not normal, we're free to exercise our suspicious, questioning judgement.

The tone of the news and current affairs programmes is calculated to allay our suspicions, to assure us, through constant repetition, that normality can only be equated with "official reality".

A spokesman of the Confederation of British Industry blames the state of the economy on the fact that the trade unions refuse to be content with a 5 per cent increase in wages. Higher wages will inevitably lead either to higher prices or reduced profits. And profits are already down to 5 per cent. Nobody could be expected to invest for a mere five per cent profit.

To question the normality of this explanation is to label yourself an eccentric.

To question the normality involves a conscious act of rejection. We have to deny the objective reality of what we're being shown, to remind ourselves continually that what we are seeing is the result of selection and editing, that it represents somebody's *choice* – a choice made by people who are seen as "responsible" by the institution that employs them.

The accepted skills of filmed reporting on television, however, are precisely those which encourage us to forget that we're seeing a manufactured product. "Professional" editing means, in Eric Morecambe's words, that "you can't see the join".

The weekly recorded highlights of football matches, on both BBC and ITV, illustrate the principle. We're *told* that they're highlights, but the selected chunks of the game that we're allowed to see are cut together so smoothly that we can never know whether we're seeing the accurate reproduction of the flow of play, or the splicing together of two separate bits of action. It's assumed that we won't want to know: that we'll prefer the illusion of being at a match rather than the awareness of the process of selection. The *technique* of the editing invites us to switch off that part of our minds that tells us we're looking through someone else's eyes, at carefully chosen passages of play, and to accept the illusion that we're experiencing the real game. (We know we're not, but for the programme to work we have to pretend we are.)

Television reportage *depends* on persuading the viewers

that seeing is believing. If you stop believing that the fires
you are seeing on the news have been produced by bombs
exploded *that afternoon*, and that the shot of a particular
snow-plough in Ayrshire (which may look suspiciously like
the shot of a snow-plough in Somerset shown two nights
earlier) is in fact a particular snow-plough in Ayrshire, then
the whole basis of television news falls apart.

The assumption that television skills involve persuading
viewers that seeing is believing is so completely taken for
granted that it's been embraced even by writers and
directors who are consciously committed to challenging
"official reality". Playwright Roy Minton, for example, in
his TV play, *Scum*, was trying to give viewers a picture of
life in Borstal which could never have emerged from (in the
words of Peter Fiddick, TV critic of the *Guardian*) "an
officially sanctioned documentary". Minton apparently
succeeded so well that the BBC banned the play on the
grounds that viewers might believe they were seeing the
"truth" about Borstal: and when Minton said they would be
(he'd interviewed between 80 and 100 people – trainees,
Borstal staff, probation officers, parents and a Borstal
Governor – and found "an overwhelming consistence of
reportage") the BBC produced two "specialists with a
knowledge and some experience of Borstals" to measure
Minton's "truth" against that of "official reality". The
experts decreed that, although all the incidents in the play
could have happened, they couldn't all have happened in
one Borstal in that space of time: to which Minton replied
that "one of the most elementary skills of the dramatist is his
ability to condense his material into a period of actual time
that will retain his audience's interest while not abusing its
credulity".

To abuse the audience's credulity could mean either to
use dramatic skills to persuade the audience to believe a lie,
or to ask the audience to accept something that's hard to
swallow. Both meanings imply that the dramatist's job is to
make people believe, to make them forget that they're seeing

a manufactured product and agree that they're seeing "reality".

But this, too, is how the makers of news and current affairs programmes see their job. Minton's version of "reality" is clearly very different from the official version. But in trying to persuade us to swallow his radical version, he (and the school of "social realist" playwrights of which he's typical) is confirming one of the central lessons of TV's hidden curriculum – if you see it on the box, it must be true.

Roy Minton has been quoted as saying, of *Scum*, that nobody "likes" it. The implication is that the play contains some "truth" that we ought to be told about, whether we "like" it or not.

But most of us switch on our television sets, not because we feel we ought to be told something, but because we want to be entertained (if the BBC had permitted us to see *Scum*, and we hadn't found it entertaining, most of us would have switched off).

Both the BBC and ITV recognise our desire to be entertained by spending much more on entertainment than on information and education. But because they're expected to be public services, both authorities talk slightingly of this major part of their output.

The Independent Television Authority, for example, in their 1969–70 annual report felt it necessary to deny that comedy and light entertainment belong "in some disreputable bargain-basement of broadcasting". Falling back on the Protestant work ethic, to justify pleasure, the ITA Report points out that "No aspect of broadcasting calls for ... harder work ... than the business of earning laughs" (comedy is O.K. because hard work is involved). Not all the programmes, the report admits, are of "the highest quality. But it would be wrong to exaggerate. Many programmes have given a great deal of pleasure to very many people."

More revealing of official attitudes, however, was the statement made by Tom Sloan in a BBC lunch-time lecture on 11 December 1969. Sloan was at that time responsible for BBC Light Entertainment: the BBC thought highly enough of his lecture to reproduce it as a pamphlet.

Sloan said:

> We have Drama and Features and Arts Features and General Features and Documentaries *and* Talks and Current Affairs, to name but a few. But I believe that a great mass of people want to treat their television sets as a means of escape, and never more so than at the present time.

> I remember one wet Sunday, in 1961, driving to Liverpool to see a new group called the Beatles give a concert for their fan club which we televised. For the first time in my life, I saw the industrial north of England, the rows of terraced houses, fronting on to the cobbled roads, glistening in the rain. The sheer ghastliness of it all was overpowering, but on the roof of every house, there was a television aerial. Antennae reaching for escape to another world. And, heaven knows, why not?

> So my job is to organise a stream of output which is primarily intended to please and relax those who wish to receive it. In other words, to entertain.

Sloan's attitude to the "great mass of people" is very similar to that of the liberal politicians who, a century earlier, introduced compulsory education. They looked out at the masses, were overpowered by the "sheer ghastliness" of what they saw, and decided that the masses needed "help". They helped them by forcing their children to go to school.

Sloan looks out of his car at the "industrial north", and is also overpowered by the "sheer ghastliness". He decides that the masses need, not "help", but "escape". So he organises for them a stream of entertainment, which is equated with relaxation.

Sloan's reference to Liverpool underlines the remoteness of a BBC executive from the way most people live. Sloan is, presumably, an "expert" on Light Entertainment, otherwise he wouldn't have been qualified for the job. Yet he shows no understanding at all of the way people in Liverpool used entertainment between his visit in 1961 and his lecture in 1969. Confronted, for the first time in his life, with the "sheer ghastliness" of the industrial north, Sloan can only assume that people want to "escape". But what made Liverpool a centre of popular culture in the 1960's was precisely the fact that large numbers of people were using the entertainment, not to escape from the assumed "ghastliness", but to celebrate the joys of being Liverpudlian.

Disc-jockey, Billy Butler, who in the early 1960's was a regular panel member on ITV's weekly pop show, *Thank Your Lucky Stars*, and who, by 1979, had become the most popular broadcaster on Radio Merseyside, recalls how an unknown young musician called George Harrison approached him in 1962 and asked him to mention on telly the equally unknown group he worked with. Billy Butler said, "You know I can't mention a group just because it comes from Liverpool" – but, years later, he commented, "Soon, Liverpool groups were at the top of everything. We'd taken over." Chicago and New Orleans had once been the world centres of popular music. They were remote, mythical cities, like Hollywood. But, suddenly, Liverpool was the centre, and the world was talking about the "Mersey sound".

And it wasn't just the pop groups who had taken over. Liverpool Football Club threatened to take over permanently as the top club in English League Football. Liverpool supporters, in one of the most inexplicable transformations ever in popular music, adopted a tear-jerking song from the American musical, *Carousel* – "When you walk through the storm keep your chin up high ..." – and turned it into an expression of communal pride: "Walk on, walk on, with hope in your heart, And you'll never walk alone ..." (Nobody who's experienced the thousands on the Anfield Kop in full voice, red scarves and banners waving slowly and majestically, could equate the experience with "escape" and "relaxation".)

And while the Beatles were making Penny Lane one of the best known streets in the world, comedian Ken Dodd was putting Knotty Ash on the map. Actors who'd spent years trying to eradicate regional accents suddenly found that they had to learn Scouse. A group of writers brought out a bestselling volume of poetry called *The Liverpool Scene*. There was no gap between their poetry and the popular entertainments. The poets performed their poetry, as singers perform songs, in the pubs and the clubs. One of the poets, Adrian Henri, wrestled publicly in mud with Alan Williams (the man who gave the Beatles away, after managing them on their first visit to Hamburg). Another poet, Roger McGough, formed a group called *The Scaffold*. Their recording of their own song, *Thank You Very Much*, reached the top of the charts, and included the mysterious line, "Thank you very much for the Aintree iron".

The fact that, after eight years of this popular ferment, the man responsible for BBC Light Entertainment could still talk of "Antennae reaching to escape to another world – and heaven knows, why not?" says a great deal about the gap between the way the broadcasting authorities see their role, and the things most of us live by.

The gap, however, has its advantages. Roy Minton's play was banned because the BBC, accepting the normal criteria of credibility, decided that the picture of Borstal was convincing enough to be taken seriously. Programmes that are offered as "mere entertainment" are more likely to get away with a lack of respect for officialdom than programmes which force the BBC to act "responsibly".

Many entertainment programmes, of course, are as vapid, frivolous, undemanding and supportive of consensus values as the news and current affairs programmes. But there are others, including some of the most popular – programmes such as *The Morecambe and Wise Show*; *The Two*

Ronnies; *Porridge*; *Till Death Do Us Part*; *Oh No, It's Selwyn Froggitt*; *The Sweeney* – which make demands on the audience and show a healthy disrespect for official pretensions.

If the information services try to teach us that "truth" is equated with a particular tone of voice, and that seeing is believing, what are the lessons of the entertainers? What do they teach *me*, night after night, as a regular viewer?

In the first place, all the programmes I've mentioned – and many others – teach a new and particular language. The language of a television series may be defined as that element in a programme which can only be fully appreciated by an audience familiar with other programmes in the series.

Sometimes the language may work through a simple gesture or catch-phrase – as when Morecambe gets a laugh by slapping Wise's cheeks: or when Selwyn Froggitt puts his thumbs up and says "Magic". (When Bill Maynard, who played Selwyn, was recognised at the 1977 Rugby League Cup Final, hundreds of spectators stuck their thumbs in the air and shouted "Magic". To anybody who didn't know the series, the ritual must have been incomprehensible.)

Sometimes the language depends on a repeated image. When Ronnie Corbett comes to the bit in *The Two Ronnies* where he sits in a chair and tells a joke, we know that the comedy is going to spring, not from the joke, but from the fact that he'll wander completely away from the story and ramble on inconsequentially before finding his way back to the punch-line. It's *how* he rambles, and *how* he gets back to the point that forms the real content of the act. But if we hadn't learnt to expect the inconsequentiality, we'd miss the point.

In a series like *Till Death Do Us Part*, the language is built round the characters and the relationship between them. The frustrated ravings of Warren Mitchell's Alf Garnett are counterpointed by the stubborn placidity of his wife, as played by Dandy Nichols (it's all water off a duck's back to her), and by the pseudo-intellectual diatribes of the son-in-law, who's tacitly supported by Alf's daughter. Writer Johnny Speight has established a pattern that he can play with. So, in one episode he gives the daughter a long, straight, impassioned speech about women's rights. The speech in itself isn't funny, but the *scene* is: simple shots of Warren Mitchell and Dandy Nichols listening to her make us laugh, because we know how they're reacting. From our familiarity with them, we read the comedy into the situation.

The language of *The Sweeney* is built round characters in action – but also round a relationship that has been created by two actors as the series has developed. The relationship between Regan and his boss, Haskins, was never written into the script. It evolved through the playing of John Thaw and Gareth Morgan, who gradually taught viewers to be aware of what was going on behind the text.

Sometimes the language of a series develops a complexity that would be esoteric but for the fact that it's known and understood by millions of viewers. In the middle of a fast-moving comic sketch, Ernie Wise coughs, and Eric Morecambe says "Arsenal" – and the audience laughs. The joke refers back to a sketch by Morecambe and Wise performed years earlier, a mock sports quiz in which Wise fed Morecambe the answers – whenever Wise coughed the correct answer was "Arsenal".

Morecambe and Wise have a sequence in which they refer explicitly to the language they've created. Wise tells the audience confidentially that Eric has become very predictable. To prove it, Wise predicts what Morecambe will do when he appears. Morecambe obliges. Wise takes Morecambe through virtually the entire repertoire of Morecambe gags, predicting what Morecambe will do next. Morecambe follows the predictions. "You're so predictable," jeers Wise. But he's forgotten one gag and the audience knows he's forgotten it. Morecambe hasn't forgotten either. He ends the sequence by slapping Wise firmly on the cheeks.

The comedy depends entirely on an assumption that the audience knows the language of the show.

The confidence which allows Morecambe and Wise to throw in the Arsenal gag, almost as an aside, and to build a comic sequence around the language of their own show, implies an attitude to the audience very different from that of the people responsible for the news and current affairs programmes.

The assumption behind the news and current affairs programmes is that we're not capable of understanding the world unless it's interpreted for us by the experts. "Phase 3 was followed by Phase 4," a commentator will patiently explain, while a ticket reading " 3" is replaced on the screen by a ticket reading "4". "But the unions have now made Phase 4 unworkable" – and he puts a big "X" across the "4" on the screen. We're talked to as if we're rather dull children who can't be expected to understand a simple statement. (Ronnie Barker, in *The Two Ronnies*, gleefully parodies the experts: "Here is a map. And here is another map. And here is a picture of a building …".)

Morecambe and Wise, on the other hand, assume that we *know* enough and are quick-witted enough to be able to take comparatively esoteric references in our stride. The confidence is based on the knowledge that there's an area of reference that regular viewers share, and that doesn't need to be explained (except to people who aren't regular viewers). The area extends beyond the language of a particular series: so that when the two Ronnies parody *Colditz*, they're drawing both on the language *they've* created (the audience has come to expect a slab of mock serial in which the two Ronnies play most of the parts) and on the language of *Colditz* itself ("I'm the Chairman of the Escape Committee," says Ronnie Barker, dead-pan, as he's let out of a lavatory he's been locked in: the parody works because of the accuracy with which the stiff-upper-lip solemnity of the original is captured).

Paul Barker, in his introduction to *Arts in Society*, defines mass art as "that which anyone can have a view on, and that view be as valid as anyone else's. Mass art is what everyone knows about."

In the context of an education system which leaves the great majority of people convinced that they're not clever enough to be expected to know much about anything, a form of communication that assumes that they *do* know, that assures them that they can be expected to understand, is itself an educational positive. It sets people up rather than putting them down. But many of the programmes I've referred to go further than that. They encourage an irreverence towards authority that, consciously or not, challenges the authoritarian attitudes on which our television services are based.

In some of the programmes I've referred to, the irreverence to authority is there, openly, in the subject matter. *Porridge*, in which Ronnie Barker plays a professional criminal in prison, could be summed up in one image: "You can't beat the system," says a prison officer, and Ronnie Barker sticks up two fingers behind the prison officer's back.

Alf Garnett, in *Till Death Do Us Part*, says all the things that authority tells us we shouldn't say. While apparently remaining unctuously loyal to traditional authoritarian values – the Queen, the Empire, the Flag – he abuses coons, wogs, women and Liverpudlians. "Official reality" tells us we're all liberals nowadays: Garnett proves that we're not. Whether people approve or disapprove of Garnett matters less than the fact that, while making us laugh, he's making us aware that there's a different reality from the one we're supposed to believe in.

The Sweeney kicks a hole through the traditional image of the police. The highly-respectable, obviously middle-class Barlow (of *Z Cars* and *Softly, Softly*) is replaced as hero by Regan, a working-class cockney, who's in there, mixing it with the hard boys. He dresses like them, talks like them, acts like them – if he weren't a cop he might well be a Kray twin. And his fight isn't only with criminals — it's with his boss, Haskins, an authority figure. *The Sweeney* invites us to identify with Regan against authority.

There's an open hostility to authority in the *content* of these programmes. But there's a more subtle demolition of "official reality" in the *form* of such series as *The Two Ronnies* and *The Morecambe and Wise Show*.

The Two Ronnies is very largely *about* the medium. The programme begins and ends with an image of two newsreaders. Ronnie Barker parodies party political broadcasts, epilogues, appeals. There's a mock-serial. And there are spectacular mock-ups of TV spectaculars. The mock-ups work because, like the parody of *Colditz*, they're accurate: Big Jim Jehosophat and Fatbelly Jones become country-and-western singers in their own right while demolishing the earnestness with which television handles country-and-western.

Morecambe and Wise conduct a regular course in anti-illusionist drama. While *Play for Today* tries to persuade us to believe what we see, while not abusing our credulity, Morecambe and Wise enlist the stars of legitimate theatre, such as Glenda Jackson, to destroy legitimate theatre conventions.

Wise writes a heroic tragedy on the death of Horatio Nelson. Lady Hamilton is played by Fenella Fielding, who confesses that she falls unresisting into the arms of any man who utters the words "Haydock Park, Oldham Athletic". Both Morecambe and Wise want to play Nelson — for a time there are two one-armed, one-eyed Nelsons on the "stage". Wise eventually persuades Morecambe to play Hardy, which Morecambe does as Robert Newton playing Long John Silver. He keeps forgetting which leg is missing, and shifts his crutch from one armpit to the other. He carries a cat on his shoulder instead of a parrot — when he takes off his cloak, the cat comes off too: it's a two-dimensional cut-out sewn on to the cloak. At the climax of the tragedy, Ernie Wise murmurs "Kiss me, Hardy." "Haydock Park,

Oldham Athletic," says Eric Morecambe, and Fenella Fielding falls unresisting into his arms.

Both material and style are anti-heroic, in popular theatre tradition. In that tradition, playwrights frequently call attention to the fact that the play is a play — Shakespeare has characters remark that if this were happening on a stage nobody would believe it. Morecambe and Wise remind us that a show is a show. "People will think we're a couple of cheap music-hall comedians," says Wise, complaining about the script. "We *are* a couple of cheap music-hall comedians," says Morecambe. "What do you think of it so far?" Morecambe asks anything that happens to be around — and the answer is always "Rubbish".

Morecambe and Wise warn us never to be taken in by appearances. The men singing "There is nothing like a dame" may *look* like sailors in an American musical: they turn out to be a collection of newsreaders. Like rude schoolboys, we've always wanted to look up Angela Rippon's skirt, but her legs have always been hidden under the newsdesk. Morecambe and Wise show her with no skirt at all. The tone of their shows is relentlessly irreverent. "I watch the Epilogue," says Morecambe reflectively. "Just in case there are a couple of good gags."

In the Journal of the Association of Assistant Librarians (December 1978) Peter Stokes, of Birmingham Central Reference Library, recalls George Orwell's prediction of the use of centralised control of language to eliminate alternative modes of thought. He asks:

> When Ms Rippon tells us about the activities of IRA "gunmen", Rhodesian "terrorists", "militant" shop stewards or "moderate" politicians, who is there to question the criteria used in constructing this controlled vocabulary?

The comedians certainly aren't doing anything as portentous as consciously questioning the criteria. They're committed to entertaining us. But the *form* of that entertainment sometimes makes it possible for us to confront what's offered as reality with a bit less credulity and a bit more awareness.

"So it's goodnight from me," says Ronnie Corbett as a newsreader. "And it's goodnight from him," says Ronnie Barker.

And for a moment the rituals of *The Nine O'Clock News* and *News at Ten* are seen for what they are: rituals.

Television teaches us that we have a right to be entertained in our own home. It also teaches us that this right can only be exercised by the grace of authority, which ordains that entertainment can only be provided as part of a public service which is legally obliged to provide us with information and education as well.

Television teaches that the information services are "serious" and "responsible". The information offered is "true" and "impartial", and is concerned with real life. Television provides an official picture of reality.

Television also teaches that entertainment has nothing to do with real life, and is simply escapist. But, happily, some of the entertainment programmes have a hidden curriculum of their own. They teach us to look with less reverence at the official version of reality that "serious" television has to offer.

Those of us who believe that education is about understanding the social environment and learning how to change it clearly have to take this hidden curriculum into account, since television is an important part of that environment for virtually everybody in our society.

We can approach the subject in two ways. First, we can use conventional academic and educational techniques to describe and analyse television – as the authors of *Bad News* and the makers of the educational series, *Viewpoint* (eventually banned by the IBA), have tried to do. But, secondly, we can take and develop the language of television entertainment itself – a language shared, understood and enjoyed by the great majority of people whom the language of conventional education has so obviously failed.

What follows is an account of one group's attempts to use the second method in order to invent new models – models which, hopefully, might be useful to people trying to change both the television and the education we've got.

PART TWO

Report on Three Projects

Open Night; Sam Spade Meets Johann Kepler;
Spies at Work

In 1975 a group of former members of the Bradford Art
College Theatre Group worked with students from the
Bradford College Community Arts course and several
groups of 16-year-old school-leavers from a number of
different schools in Bradford to make three videotapes aimed
at using the language of popular entertainment for a
conscious educational purpose.

For the seven previous years the Bradford Art College
Theatre Group had been developing a method of learning
through theatre, and had also been developing a form of
theatre which tried to communicate information through
entertainment. Sometimes the Group had helped to create
events in which large numbers of people took an active part
– as when, for a week, working with students, they re-
created, in the Serpentine Gallery in a London park, the
building of the Union Pacific Railway. Sometimes they used
the idiom of popular movies to make shows for people who
never normally went to the theatre – as when they presented
the Cuban Missile Crisis as a Western being made by John
Ford. In turning to video, the Group were trying to use the
methods they'd developed in theatre as the basis for
television programmes.

The three videotapes were *Open Night*, *Sam Spade Meets
Johannes Kepler* and *Spies at Work*.

Project One : Open Night

Open Night is a video entertainment about compulsory education in England. It was made as a conscious answer to Granada's educational TV series, *Open Day*.

The *Open Day* series was intended to give parents information about new developments in secondary education. But, while claiming to talk about the new, the form of the series seemed to me to reinforce acceptance of the old.

The series was held together by a narrator, who, like a teacher, conducted the viewers from one topic to another. He confirmed what both schools and television teach us to accept : that we can only hope to understand the world if it's interpreted for us by experts. The topics themselves read like subjects on a school timetable – "Curriculum Development", "Pastoral Care", "Teachers", "Money". The sense of a school timetable was strengthened by the ringing of a bell to punctuate different sections inside each programme. This, said the form, is how knowledge may normally be expected to reach us, in little bits, each different bit being signalled by the ringing of a bell.

The series, too, offered an example of what the Glasgow University Research Group which produced *Bad News* described as "limiting the agenda". For example, pupils were asked what kind of teachers they liked. The replies, selected by the programme's producer, stressed "control" linked with "understanding".

So, a girl is presented as saying, "I think teachers should be able to control the class without being absolutely too strict." A boy talks of liking teachers "that can keep control of the class" and can "get you to work without shouting at you". Another boy likes teachers "that can control the class, but are friendly and have got a good personality". Yet another girl likes teachers "that can handle children, as some children obviously get out of hand" – this last girl adds, "Because ... we're very adolescent, and we need teachers that can understand us."

The picture presented is one of young people who recognise that they need to be controlled by teachers: all they ask is that the teachers should control them with understanding.

Bradford school-leavers, talking amongst themselves in front of our video cameras, revealed a much less co-operative attitude to teachers and to schools. They were the first group who'd been forced, by law, to stay at school until they were sixteen, and they deeply resented the fact. "So there we all were," says a girl, "all that didn't leave at fifteen. So we all turned round and said, Well, that's it. We're not doin' owt. Why should we have to stop an extra year? Why pick this year to change it all?" Commenting on the decision to raise the school-leaving age ("You should have had a vote. You should have asked the schoolchildren to vote. It's us stoppin' on school an extra year, not the people that's made the decision"), a girl says, "It's a decision they don't want. They want to leave when they're good and ready. And if they want to stay on, well, let 'em. Just let 'em make their own decisions after 15. At 16 you're allowed to get pregnant. Nobody can do owt about it."

The difference in the attitudes of the two groups of young people arises from the fact that the Granada interviewers never allowed on to the agenda the question of whether the young people wanted to be at school or not. *Open Day*'s agenda was based on a number of hidden assumptions. Assuming that you're forced to go to school whether you want to or not, assuming that when you're there you're grouped, for administrative reasons, into large, potentially unruly classes, with a teacher in charge, assuming that the teacher is given the job of teaching subjects you don't particularly want to learn, but success in which, you've been led to believe, will help you to get a better job when you leave – what kind of teachers do you like? Naturally, the ones who can control a class without too much unpleasantness, and who can get you to do the work you don't want to do without shouting at you.

As well as confirming old ways of looking, and limiting the agenda, the *Open Day* series dramatically demonstrated the contradictions in which "educational television" can find itself trapped. The strength of television as an educational weapon lies potentially in the fact that it's a mass medium. A programme giving information about secondary education can, technically, reach virtually every parent in the country.

But the mass audience watches television to be entertained. And the great majority of the mass audience is made up of people who left school as soon as they legally could. Education is something they've failed at. They don't want to re-live the experience. As Goering is supposed to have reached for his pistol when he heard the word culture, the great majority of people reach for the off-switch when they hear the word "education".

The TV authorities tacitly recognise this, when they plan their programmes. *Open Day* was put out on Sunday mornings. The only audience it could hope to attract would consist of a minority of the minority of parents already interested in secondary schools. But those already interested would be those who already have access to information about education; in other words, those who needed the programmes least.

Through its form, and the way it defined itself, the *Open Day* series inevitably cut itself off from that section of the population which most needed any information the series could succeed in giving.

In thinking about our counter-programme, *Open Night*, we agreed that we wanted to make a programme which *wouldn't* be switched off by audiences familiar with *Morecambe and Wise, The Two Ronnies, Porridge, Monty Python, The Last of the Summer Wine*. We were ourselves, of course, caught in a contradiction. There was no possibility that a programme like the one we were devising would be shown at peak viewing time. But since we were constructing a model we worked with that kind of slot and that kind of audience in mind.

Moreover, in thinking about popular television language, we didn't refer in our minds to these particular programmes simply because they were popular. One of the things that made these and other programmes popular was a sense of irreverence. The playwright, John Arden, once commented that, as seen in their popular ballads, English people over the centuries have appeared as remarkably violent and hostile to government. This hostility still shows itself, in a watered-down way, in a section of TV comedy, which thrives on scepticism — towards authority, towards pomposities and pretensions of all kinds, towards the humourless assumptions of "official reality". In trying to make an entertainment programme, we wanted to use the irreverent, popular forms as a way of looking, sceptically, at assumptions about our education system. The questioning content shaped the irreverent form.

Open Night was made by seven people: three former members of the Bradford Art College Theatre Group (Keith Knowles, Chris Vine and Roger Simcox), two students from the Community Arts course (Carol Crowe and Rodney Challis), a former Community Arts student who had become a lecturer (Ken Sparne), and myself. We did everything (except the final editing) between us — one of our aims was to demonstrate that it's possible for a small group of people to make entertaining video without becoming dependent on studio technicians. We played with the equipment as the Goons must have played with a tape-recorder when they were inventing the original Goon Shows.

Our equipment was rudimentary. We had two black-and-white cameras with monitors, a playback monitor, a mixer, a tape-deck and one microphone. We had virtually no lighting and no control box — every time we cut from one camera to the other the mixer gave a loud click. We incorporated the click into the recording and hoped that it would work as a Brechtian alienation device, reminding viewers that they were watching a videotape.

The room wasn't soundproofed. We hung the mike from the ceiling and switched it on to automatic. If anybody shouted too loud, the sound automatically cut back and the next few words came across very quietly. But when we showed the finished tape, nobody ever complained about the technical quality. The arguments were always about content.

One of the biggest problems we faced was that of inventing our own television language. Television language is mainly about familiarity: it's built up through repetition of situations, gags, relationships , over weeks, months, years. We were faced with the need to create a language that would be surprising and entertaining, but that could be quickly learnt, and, above all, could carry the content.

We began by inventing a number of video games.

There was, for example, what we called a "random cutting" game. It involved two cameras and two players. Each player sat on a chair in front of one camera. The players, each looking straight into the camera, then invented a dialogue with each other. But the dialogue was controlled by chance. The rule was that you only spoke if the camera you were looking into was recording. When your camera switched off, and the other camera switched on, that was the signal for the other person to start answering you. The switching from one camera to the other and back again was controlled by a third person at the mixer. He, or she, sat at the mixer, not listening to the dialogue, but turning up playing cards, one by one, that were face downwards in a pack. Every time a picture card was turned up, the mixer switched from one camera to the other. So the dialogue was controlled by the playing cards. The aim of the players was to catch each other out, to make each other dry up or speak out of turn.

We discovered that turning the invention of dialogue into a game freed people from all kinds of television conventions. In straight interviews, for example, schoolchildren tended to

talk, in front of the cameras, like TV presenters: they used
phrases like, "In this day and age ..." and took care to
voice the correct pious sentiments. Playing the game,
concentrating, not on making the right impression, but on
the fun of the situation, they felt free to be themselves instead
of trying to be Robin Day. So, a thirteen-year-old boy,
who, in a videoed "discussion" ("We're here tonight to talk
about whether hanging should be brought back or finally
abolished") had made statements like, "Hanging is used
today because of increasing violence amongst youths and
robbers and burglars", used quite different language when
talking about school in the random cutting game: "You're
always getting us detention. Boys always get done when
we're with you girls. It weren't us who were messing about.
Cannon were cheeking Bolus and we were getting done
summat bad."

When we first invented the random cutting game, we used
very simple situations: one player would try to sell another a
Bible, or an elephant, or three dozen crates of Newcastle
Brown ale. But, later, Keith Knowles, Chris Vine, Roger
Simcox and Ken Sparne began to take a basic story line and
build up a short video play composed of six or more
successive dialogues improvised through random cutting. In
one, Vine was a headmaster, threatening to send Simcox
back to Borstal unless he informed on his classmates.
Simcox went back to tell one of his classmates, Keith
Knowles, what the headmaster had said. Together, they
invented useless information for Simcox to tell Headmaster
Vine. Vine rejected the information and asked for something
a bit more solid. In the meantime, Knowles had a row with
the school caretaker, Ken Sparne. Knowles and Simcox
invented a way of shopping Sparne: Simcox reported
imaginary misdemeanours by Sparne to Vine. In a final
dialogue Vine sacked Sparne. (Keith Knowles had invented
the scenario: it was based on an episode from a novel by
Solzhenitsyn.)

After we'd played it out in a school situation, we did it

again as if it were happening in Colditz, with Vine as the German Camp Commandant, Knowles as a British officer, and Sparne as a camp guard. (We got the Colditz images from a sixteen-year-old girl, who, when we asked her, while she was working the camera during the making of a video story, what she thought of school, replied in one word: "Colditz".) Finally, we mixed the two ideas. Vine talked to Simcox as if they were in a school: Simcox and Knowles talked together as if they were prisoners in Colditz: and when Sparne talked to Knowles, Knowles insisted that he was a British officer, but Sparne, who behaved as if he were a school caretaker, treated Knowles as if he were a schoolboy ... Building improvisations around the random cutting game turned out to be a very useful way of getting lines for a script, and also of inventing characters and building up relationships between them. All the characters invented in the School/Colditz improvisation re-appeared in *Open Night*.

As well as playing with words, we played with objects. As soon as the mixer switched on a camera, the person in front of the camera had to use an everyday object in an unusual way. Vine picked up a piece of cable and began to make elaborate shapes with it: the cable became an image of technological equipment in *Open Night*. Roger Simcox used a fire-extinguisher as a huge gun: that, too, became a recurring gag in *Open Night*. Rodney Challis used a chair as a hammer to try and knock a block of wood into the wall. The chair used as a hammer appeared several times in the final videotape.

We played a "hide the thimble" game in which a group of people with paper bags on their heads searched around the room for a thimble while the video camera followed them. In *Open Night* we presented schoolchildren as creatures with paper bags over their heads.

We had a Headmaster of the Year competition. The competitors took it in turn to make statements, to the camera, that they'd heard headmasters make in School Assembly. The one who could remember the most statements and deliver them with suitable solemnity won the competition. And we developed a number of improvisations around the line, "I would have done my homework, but ...". Looking into camera one, a player would say, "I would have done my homework, but, last night, on my way home from school, I was sitting next to this little old lady on the bus and ...". Then he'd move in front of camera two, and join a second player. The second player would have to become the little old lady and invent a way of destroying the homework.

While we were inventing the video games, we were working for much of the time with volunteer groups of school-leavers. They helped us invent more games. They made videotapes in which still images were set at random against a written commentary. One group scripted and taped a mock, slightly obscene version of *This Is Your Life*. We had the groups for a week at a time, and nearly every group, at some stage in the week, went through a period when they told dirty jokes and sang dirty songs on the video. They'd look at us to see when we would interfere. When we didn't, they'd push the jokes even further. But when it finally dawned on them that we really weren't going to stop them, their interest in shocking soon began to flag and they went on to other things. (I was always mildly worried that some Mrs. Whitehouse of a teacher would see the tapes and get the projects closed down — but if we had used our position to censor them, the attempt to create an open working situation would have broken down.)

In between the games and improvisations, they talked, with the video cameras openly switched on. They talked to each other about their different schools. They talked about being "lumped" into classrooms, left to listen to the radio or read comics, of teachers and pupils bashing each other, of

the police being called in, of common rooms wrecked —
"We ruined it for ourselves. We had a vending machine for
coffee till we smashed it up." They were a bit bewildered by
their own violence. Most of them wanted to get away from
school — but the only way they could escape was by getting
themselves suspended. That would go against them when
they went for a job. "So it's best just to sit in back of class
and do nowt."

They invented a way of making collective cartoons on
video. One group drew a cartoon of a school and then burnt
it.

While we were playing video games and making tapes
with school-leavers, we were also reading up on educational
history. We were looking for a central image around which
we could build our programme. We found it in G. A. N.
Lowndes' *The Silent Social Revolution* — "an account of
the expansion of public education in England and Wales
1895–1935".

Lowndes' book, first published in 1937, is one of the
accepted key texts dealing with the history of compulsory
education. In the early chapters, Lowndes paints a grim
picture of life in England in the second half of the nineteenth
century before the introduction of Forster's 1870 Education
Act. As well as Dostoevsky's picture of London (already
cited on p 11), which Lowndes accepts as if it were objective
fact, he quotes, again as an objective description, an account
of an early State school:

> They were a wild lot gathered in the Willow Alley shed. Not
> one boy had experienced any but parental discipline before,
> and most of the little fellows had been used to blows. When
> the teacher spoke to a lad the youngster's hands were
> instinctively made ready to protect the head. Their minds
> were in a turmoil; their curiosity was at fever pitch. Some
> were hardy enough; some were cowed and sly but vicious,
> and some were dulled into semi-imbecility by hunger,

disease, ill-usage. They had no conception of the meaning of an order and the teacher was obliged to drill them again and again in the simplest movements ... They had the fluid mind of the true barbarian and it was quite useless to attempt any species of coercion.

In both these descriptions, which Lowndes accepts as objective, middle-class writers look at working-class people with a mixture of fascination, disgust and fear. Lowndes accepts the belief that the introduction of State education involved a civilising process. He quotes an Inspector:

"Of one thing I am quite sure," wrote Mr. Sharpe, Senior Chief Inspector, referring to London in 1895, "that so far as their teaching goes it is thoroughly intelligent and practical, but it rests with the generation 10 or 15 years hence to pronounce how far it has been successful in training English men and women for their lives' work."

Lowndes goes on without any sense of irony:

One wonders if he lived to see the triumphant vindication of his London elementary schools by the London battalions in the withering machine-gun fire at Gommecourt, in the desperate resistance at Cambrai and Gavrelle, on the sun-scorched plain at Gaza and in the mud of Glencorse Wood.

Lowndes notes, with apparent approval, that after twenty years of compulsory education a potentially violent, anarchic, undisciplined mob has been turned into an unquestioning, highly disciplined army, willing to die bravely and heroically if they are ordered to do so by representatives of the State which has "educated" them. ("The manhood of Britain today," wrote A. S. Neill in *A Dominie Dismissed* in 1920, "has passed through the schools; they have been lulled to sleep ... Train a boy to obey his teacher and he will naturally obey every dirty politician who has the faculty of rhetoric ...".)

Lowndes, in fact, uses a military metaphor to describe attitudes to children in 1870. He notes that people accepted that

> the primary concern of the State in discharging the new responsibilities it had undertaken must be to afford to this army of children a militia training directed to the acquisition of quite general powers such as the arts of speech, reading and writing and the fundamental ideas of magnitude and number. A militia, it was recognised, must be supplemented by a small professional army; and this must have received post-primary education.

Lowndes' military metaphor, coupled with his acceptance that compulsory education helped to prepare men to die unquestioningly in the First World War, offered us our own central image. The compelling of children to go to school amounted to an act of conscription. Children were grouped together in schools as conscripted soldiers were grouped together in camps. Teachers were put in charge of children as officers and guards were put in charge of soldiers.

"What's school like?" "Colditz."

Putting people forcibly into camps became a central image of *Open Night*.

Open Night begins with three authority figures, Knowles, Vine and Simcox, making video pictures. Knowles is clearly the boss: he's a mixture of blustering headmaster and R.A.F. officer. Vine and Simcox are like two favourite pupils, vying for his attention: but Vine is aggressive – he refers to people as "unprepossessing yobs" – while Simcox is ingratiating: "What do you think, *sir*?" Vine makes a picture of a young man (Rodney Challis) using a chair as a hammer to knock a block of wood into the wall. "That's the kind of unprepossessing yob who runs up and down on Saturday afternoons chucking bricks through windows," he comments. He makes a picture of a woman (Carol Crowe).

She's making shapes out of a piece of cable. "No idea how to use modern technology," says Vine.

Simcox suggests giving the creatures speech. Rodney describes how his father was a school caretaker, how he went to Grammar School and won a scholarship to University, then came back to teach at his old Grammar School. "Ignorant yob," says Vine.

The woman describes how, when her son first went to Grammar School, she enjoyed helping him with his homework. She got "fair excited", she says, by the mathematics. "Fair excited!" exclaims Simcox. "That's not proper English!" "Pity nobody told her about that accent," says Vine, in broad Yorkshire. Soon, says the woman sadly, she couldn't understand what her son was doing any more. She felt bewildered and lost. "Shows a certain verbal aptitude," says Simcox. "Not much sign of disciplined thought," comments Knowles.

Simcox asks Knowles to explain the pictures. Knowles hazards a guess that the creatures on the screen are trying to talk, in a gibbering sort of way, about education. He tells Vine to put on an educational documentary about English education in 1870. There's a quick shot of a man with his head in a paper bag confronted by another man who uses a fire-extinguisher as a gun. "Socrates," says this second man, "you are found guilty of committing genuine education": and he shoots dead the figure in the paper bag. "You idiot, Vine," says Knowles. "You're three thousand years out." "It wasn't my fault," says Vine. "The machine ..." "The machine never lies," says Knowles, as a picture of modern New York appears on the screen and a Walter Winchell-type commentator says, "London, England, 1870".

The rest of *Open Night* consists of tapes within tapes. The convention is established by the use of the Walter Winchell-type narrator. Walter Winchell used to give a pseudo-documentary commentary to the American TV cop series, *The Untouchables*, creating the impression that what viewers were seeing was a reconstruction of "fact". We used the commentary deliberately to point out that what documentaries normally ask us to believe is objective fact is really a particular way of looking. We offered a different way of looking.

> In the 1800's, sometimes known as the nineteenth century, organised crime was changing the face of the English countryside. Mobsters, such as coal-owners, ironmasters and woollen manufacturers, were spawning dens of vice known as – factories. Peasants, who for centuries had been left free to starve in peace in the green countryside, now found themselves starving on black city streets. Copulation was rife. The murky job of passing on useless information to the young had previously been left to informers, known as – schoolmasters, hired by the rival gangs. The gang with the largest body of paid informers was a mob of property speculators and slum landlords, known as – the Church of England.

The first tape within a tape – *The Unteachables: An Educational Documentary* – deals with the introduction of compulsory education. Knowles, Vine and Simcox appear as members of a cabinet – Simcox announces himself as Forster. They're clearly the same characters who have previously been inventing video pictures. They wear gangster hats.

Simcox is perturbed:

SIMCOX. It's the children, sir. As I've been going up and down the country making money, I can't help noticing that there are a lot of children everywhere. They're all barefoot, sir, running wild all over the streets, hanging around the doors of public houses. I can't stand it, sir. I fall over their weak and frail bodies as I'm going into the Reform Club for dinner. The pain of it's driving me mad.

KNOWLES. Pull yourself together, Simcox. Remember who you are.

SIMCOX. The name's Forster, sir.
KNOWLES. Ah, yes. Forster, Simcox.

Knowles observes that they can't have children littering the streets. Gives the country a bad name. "Fetch me a map of the world," he says. "We'll start a war somewhere. Send them all into the trenches." Vine points out that they're not old enough to go in the army. "Send them up the chimneys," says Knowles. "Down the mines." Simcox explains that there aren't enough chimneys to go round. "And they're too small to go down the mines. They only get under their mothers' feet." Vine triumphantly suggests compulsory education for all children between five and eleven.

Knowles is shocked. "Compulsory education? The British people will never stand for that! An Englishman's home is his castle and all that." "But most of them ain't got no homes," shouts Simcox: and Vine adds, "We haven't got any schools either, but we can build those, and in the meantime we can hold classes under railway arches." "Good thinking, Vine," says Knowles – but as he wanders out he's still muttering, "Compulsory education! What an unthinkable thought!"

We wanted to use, throughout the programme, a comic trio that we established as clearly as the Marx Brothers or the Three Stooges, to offer a way of looking at compulsory education that would make viewers question established beliefs. We hoped that viewers, while laughing, would protest, "But they didn't *really* introduce compulsory education to get kids off the streets!" And then go on to wonder, "Or did they?"

Introducing the next sequence, the Walter Winchell commentary tells us that at first children put up a spirited resistance, but that soon School Boards were given the power to search and apprehend.

Beside a fireplace, under the motto "Home Sweet

Home", a mother (Carol Crowe) is drinking gin and playing cards with her son (Rodney Challis). There's a knock at the door. "Quick! It's the School Board", says the mother. She hides cards, gin and Rodney, and starts knitting. Vine enters, wearing a gangster-hat and carrying the fire-extinguisher. "Don't take him," begs the mother, and makes an impassioned speech (taken, in fact, from a letter written to a School Board office by a distressed mother, and quoted by Lowndes):

> His father is 60 years of age and he goes 4 miles every morning and 4 miles back, that makes 8 miles a day, and if it is fine so he can work on the farm he gets 14s., but if it is wet he cannot work, and there's 4s. rent and 4 children to keep in food and clothes, no wonder the farmers do not prosper, and this cruel, cruel law of the School Board ...

"What cruel, cruel law?" asks Vine. "It's for his own good, ma'am. We've come to *civilise* him. Come on, you ignorant pig," and he leads Rodney out at gunpoint.

Once again we were using a parody of a popular form – this time the cop show – in an attempt to make a serious point: that the introduction of compulsory education *was* seen at the time as an intrusion on family rights, and did cause real problems.

In the final sequence of this first tape within a tape, Simcox and Vine demonstrate how teachers prepared "English men and women for their lives' work". First, Simcox drills Vine "again and again in the simplest movements": "Put your hands in the air. Now put them down again. Put them up. Put them down. Up. Down. Up ...". Next Vine's "life's work" is demonstrated. Vine sits with his head in a paper bag: Simcox, using the fire-extinguisher, shoots him dead. "One wonders if the Senior Chief inspector lived to see the triumphant vindication of his London elementary schools by the London battalions in the withering machine-gun fire at Gommecourt

...", the Walter Winchell commentary speculates, adding: "The machine never lies ...".

These early sequences in *Open Night* are used, not only to tell a story and give information, but to introduce a language. The language is made up of the physical appearance of the performers — particularly the three central figures, who quickly become familiar — and of the consistency of the characters they've created; of the use of the Walter Winchell-type commentary; and of the constant re-appearance of familiar objects used in a particular way — the chair used as a hammer, the fire-extinguisher used as a gun, the paper bags put on the heads of victims. Throughout the rest of the tape, a pattern is developed.

For example, the sequence introducing the 1944 Education Act begins with a Walter Winchell-type commentary which parallels the earlier 1870 sequence:

Between 1939 and 1945 gang warfare spread across the surface of the planet earth. The leaders of the rival gangs ordered all able-bodied males to be abducted and trained as hit-men. Their job — murder. During the long periods of inactivity, the hit-men were kept in camps, watched over by guards known as — army officers, belonging either to the enemy gang or to their own.

The chair used as a hammer re-appears in a sequence which refers to the TV comedy series, *Billy Liar*, and so does the fireplace and the image of "Home Sweet Home". The sequence opens with a shot of an army hut. The camera zooms in to the door. Inside there's the fireplace, and "Home Sweet Home", and the mother knitting. But the son is using a chair as a hammer to knock a block of wood against the wall. "What are you doing now, our Billy?" asks the mother (Carol Crowe). "I'm trying to find a way of escaping from this prison camp," says the boy (Rodney Challis). "It's all those war films you've been watching," says the mother. "And I'll not have you calling our little semi-detached a prison camp."

In the *Billy Liar* sequence, we introduced another everyday object that became part of *Open Night*'s language – a ladder. Knowles, Vine and Simcox sit watching Rodney trying to escape from his "prison camp". "The trouble with this war," says Vine, "is that there's too much inactivity. Unprepossessing yobs like that have too much time on their hands. They're beginning to get themselves educated." "Educated!" cries Simcox in alarm. "But isn't that dangerous? What are we going to do?" Vine suggests sending a ladder down the chimney. "Good thinking, Vine," says Knowles. "Simcox: nip down and talk to the bounder."

Rodney is still trying to knock a hole in the wall. His father (Ken Sparne, playing a school caretaker) says, "He should put some coal on that fire." He's referring to what's obviously a two-dimensional charcoal drawing on a huge sheet of paper. Suddenly, a ladder begins to come down from the top of the screen. Both mother and father ignore it. "The trouble with our Billy," says the father, as the ladder appears, "is that he's living in a bloody dream world." Simcox climbs down the ladder, tells Rodney that he's good officer material, and invites Rodney to follow him back up. Rodney's head disappears off the top of the screen in one shot, and appears at the bottom of the screen, in the room where Knowles and Vine are sitting, in the next shot. After answering a few routine questions ("What were the main characteristics of the Renaissance?", "Who spoke the line, 'To be or not to be …'?", "What were the main causes of the French Revolution?"), Rodney is given a degree, a gangster hat. Then he's sent back down the ladder while the three authority figures decide what to do with him. "Who gave certificates to all them yobs in the army?" Vine wants to know. "After the war they'll all be wanting to run prison camps, and there won't be any prison camps to run." "I'll think of something," says Simcox – and he comes up with the idea of secondary education for all.

Another sequence puts together the ladder, the fire-extinguisher and the image of the paper bags. Challis stands at the foot of the ladder, wearing his newly acquired gangster hat and pointing the fire-extinguisher at three figures who are kneeling facing a wall, with paper bags on their heads. Simcox addresses them.

SIMCOX. You men have been found guilty of being eleven years old. You're condemned to remain in camps until you're fifteen – it's called secondary education for all ... Now I know some of you have been anxious to get out into civvy street and make a packet. That's because you've not always been in camps most suited to your age, aptitude and ability. All that's going to change in the future. In the interests of preserving unity of purpose, I have devised three different kinds of camp. And in order to decide which camp is most suited to you personally, Lieutenant Challis here is going to put to you a perfectly routine question.

RODNEY. Write a letter to your Indian gardener telling him tactfully why you are forced to dispense with his services. Number One!

ONE. But I haven't got a garden.

SIMCOX. Total lack of verbal aptitude. Secondary Modern material. That doesn't mean you're a failure, Number One. It's simply that you're stupid.

RODNEY. Number Two!

TWO. Dear Mr. Ram Jam Singh: I've sold you and bought a lawn-mower.

SIMCOX. Technical institution for you. But don't imagine that makes you a success. It's simply that you're less stupid than Number One.

RODNEY. Number Three!

THREE. Dear Sir: I regret to inform you that owing to inflationary pressures entirely beyond my control ...

SIMCOX. Officer material without a doubt. Could become

Prime Minister. Grammar School for you, my boy. Take
him up the ladder, Lieutenant Challis.

The question Rodney put to the eleven-year-olds was not
in fact taken from an eleven-plus paper. But it *was* taken
from a G.C.E. "O" level English paper. Later in the video,
after Labour Education Minister, Crosland, has announced
that "from now on all secondary schools will be called
Comprehensive, and there will be an end to all this
segregation", the three figures in paper bags once again
appear at the foot of the ladder with Lt. Challis:

ONE. But I haven't got a garden.
RODNEY. Non-academic stream for you.
TWO. I've sold you and bought a lawn-mower.
RODNEY. Technical stream for you.
THREE. Problems of cash flow leading to ...
RODNEY. Follow me up the ladder ...

The ladder offers a way out for the few who make it. It
also offers a way down for those above to communicate with
the majority below. A member of the Black Paper
paratroopers (Kingsley Amis, represented by Keith
Knowles) comes down the ladder to defend academic
traditions against the mob. His Oxford University education
in English Literature, he says, has made him the world
famous novelist he is today. He offers a snatch of dialogue
between a girl and a boy who are talking about making love
("It was so absolutely non-horrible that it was nearly very
very nice." "From now on it'll be better and better"), and
comments, "You don't learn to write prose like that, you
know, without studying *Beowulf*."

Later, Simcox ("the name's Bullock, sir, Alan Bullock")
comes down the ladder to investigate illiteracy. The mother
sits at the foot of the ladder and Simcox tells her, "I know

these parent-teacher meetings can be a bit gruelling for those involved. But it's important that we should appear to be concerned. I want you to relax. Talk to me as if I were down on your level" – and he shines a bright light in her eyes as he makes her read from a school primer. He's testing her ability to recognise implicit meanings, he tells her. She reads, "Peter and Jane live in a big house. Daddy goes to work in a big car. Mummy stays at home to look after Peter and Jane. She goes shopping in a little car."

The chair, used as a hammer, re-appears in the tape's final sequence. This last tape within a tape is demonstrating what is "new" in education, "the new activity methods". Vine is doing the demonstration. He's told to pretend to be a tree. "It's autumn. Your leaves are falling, your branches are drooping ..." He looks in some anxiety at his crotch. "Now on to the next lesson. Playing with objects. I'm going to give you a chair and a piece of wood and I want you to use them *imaginatively*. No. The chair's not to sit on. Use it *imaginatively*." Vine uses the chair to hammer the block of wood against a wall. "That's very good," comments the teacher. "Now when the bell goes I want you to be ready for the next lesson." The bell goes, and Vine recites, " 'Tis now the very witching time of night ..." (He's recited it three times already while demonstrating the way syllabuses differ from one type of school to another ...) The "new activity methods" are presented as part of an educational structure which has changed, in its essentials, very little since Forster first announced his intention to "help" working-class children in 1870.

Open Night was designed for a large popular audience. But, given the television we've got, there was no way that the programme could reach a large popular audience. We showed it to groups as and when we could – to parent-teacher groups, groups of education students, community groups, adult education groups.

Many of the people in the groups came inevitably from

precisely those sections of the community which have always seen working-class young people as belonging to a "mob". Headmasters and older teachers in particular were often angry about both style and content. But it often emerged, in discussion, that the same individuals were contemptuous of popular television, anyway, and had never seen programmes like *The Untouchables* and *Billy Liar*. A number of younger teachers, on the other hand, particularly those working in inner-city schools, were enthusiastic, even when they felt that they themselves had been held up to inspection. A young, radical drama teacher said he'd been laughing happily at targets that had been hit in the tape when he suddenly found himself a target. He'd discovered himself laughing at one of his own drama exercises – "I want you to imagine you're a tree ...". But, he said, he'd found it exhilarating to be able to laugh at himself.

Working-class parents sometimes responded very strongly to particular images. In a Derbyshire mining village, for example, a teacher objected to the way the tape linked teachers with middle-class attitudes. The teachers at that particular school, he said, all lived in the village, were all part of the one village community. A woman who'd taken no part at all in the discussion suddenly spoke very quietly. Teachers were part of the village community, she agreed. But when she steeled herself to go to a parent-teachers' meeting she felt exactly like that mother at the foot of the ladder being interrogated under a strong light.

In Bradford we showed the tape to a group of mothers we knew on a council house estate. They laughed a lot, but there wasn't much discussion afterwards, until they all broke up and had cups of tea. Then two of them came and said how much they'd been affected by the scene in which the three figures had knelt at the foot of the ladder with paper bags on their heads. And they described the tensions they and their children had experienced at the time of the eleven-plus exams. "That's exactly how I felt," one of them said, referring back to the scene. Neither they nor the woman in the mining village *analysed* the images in conventional media appreciation terms. But they recognised the truth of images – even though the images were not in any way "documentary".

The value of *Open Night*, as I saw it, lay in three directions. First, we'd demonstrated that it was possible for a group of people with very limited resources to make their own video *entertainment*. (Most groups I knew were simply using video either to record events, such as rock concerts, or to do documentary interviews. We hoped that *Open Night* would encourage groups to experiment with entertainment – including groups of enthusiasts in schools, who might be able to lay their hands on the school equipment outside class time.) Secondly, we'd demonstrated that an entertainment form could be used in video to make a strong political statement. We hoped that some people in community or political groups would be encouraged to try and use video in the same way. Thirdly, we'd invented a language which could be used to comment on wide areas of "official reality". In *Open Night* the three authority figures had concentrated on solving the "education problem". It seemed to me that, in a series, they might also offer "solutions" for unemployment, immigration, Northern Ireland ... So that entertainment could be used consciously to undermine the "official" attitudes *unconsciously* asserted in the TV information services.

The extension and use of such a language depends on the people who control the television we've got. All we could do was offer a model. Which is what, we hope, *Open Night* turned out to be.

Project Two: Sam Spade meets Johann Kepler

We'd committed ourselves in the *Open Night* project to making a videotape in response to an educational television series. In the second project we were committed to taking a subject that would be acceptable in terms of conventional education and to exploring what would happen if we tried to present that subject in the language of popular entertainment.

We selected an episode in the history of science. We chose it because we already had an image in mind that was drawn from old movies — the kind of old movies that continue to attract large TV audiences.

We took, as a basic text, Arthur Koestler's account in *The Sleepwalkers* of Kepler's discovery of the laws which laid the foundation of modern physics. Koestler rejects the conventional image of the scientist as a cool, rational man, working his way logically from one hypothesis to another. Koestler sees the true innovator in science as a man driven by passion for an idea. Both passion and idea may be irrational. The discoverer moves from one guess to another in a trance-like state, stumbling on the laws of nature like a sleepwalker in a dream.

To Koestler, the 16th century scientist, Johann Kepler, is a perfect example of the sleepwalker. Consumed by a passion for proving that the universe is the embodiment of a divine harmony, Kepler stumbles, in his search for that harmony, on the laws governing planetary motion. Even the details of his search offer Koestler evidence of sleepwalking. Kepler himself describes how, at the beginning of a series of calculations about the orbit of the planet Mars, he makes a simple mathematical error. Towards the end of the calculations, he makes another error: and "these two errors — it is like a miracle — cancel out in the most precise manner". When, after a seven-year battle with the orbit of Mars, he stumbles "entirely by chance" on two figures that relate to each other, he writes, "I felt as if I had been awakened from a deep sleep!" adding, "Oh, what a foolish bird I had been!"

We intended to offer, as an image of the sleepwalker, Raymond Chandler's popular detective, Philip Marlowe. For Marlowe also contradicted a conventional image. According to the conventional image, a detective, rationally and logically, gathers together clues, examines them carefully, and comes up with a reasonable solution. But Marlowe operates much more like one of Koestler's sleepwalkers. He stumbles from one guess to another. We intended to present Kepler as Philip Marlowe. But when we began working on the videotape, we, too, stumbled on an idea.

Kepler's passion for discovering the truth about planetary orbits came from a conviction that the distances between the planets were in some way related to the special relationships of the five perfect solids when they were fitted one inside the other. He devised a drinking cup, made up of the five perfect solids, "which would then be a true and genuine likeness of the world and model of creation in so far as human reason may fathom." Kepler made a paper model of this cosmic cup for Frederick, the Duke of Würtemberg, whom Kepler was cultivating as a patron. The plan was to make the cup, encrusted with jewels, but after years of negotiation the project fell through and the cup was never made.

The picture of the proposed "cosmic cup", though, reminded someone in our group of another priceless object, which figures in one of the most popular Hollywood detective movies, John Huston's *The Maltese Falcon*. The Maltese Falcon is an antique bird, made of gold and encrusted with jewels. The search for the bird brings a gang of crooks, played by stars including Sidney Greenstreet and Peter Lorre, into contact, not with Philip Marlowe, but with another private eye of the same period, Dashiell Hammett's Sam Spade (played in the movie by Humphrey Bogart).

We decided to do our own re-make of Huston's movie, with the Cosmic Cup replacing the Maltese Falcon, and Kepler replacing the Peter Lorre figure (who came to Sam Spade in search of the falcon).

Hence, the final title: *Sam Spade Meets Johann Kepler.*

Same Spade Meets Johann Kepler was made by four of the

group that made *Open Night* (Chris Vine, Roger Simcox, Ken Sparne and myself); two other former members of the Bradford Art College Theatre Group (Ian Taylor and Maurice Burgess); and two community arts students, Larraine Hudson and Paul Kerrigan. We now had three cameras instead of two: we worked in a bare studio that had once been a bar in a huge, rambling old hotel.

Although, ostensibly, we were trying to produce an entertainment that would give scientific information, we were aiming to work on a more complex problem. We wanted to produce a videotape that could, in its form, question assumptions about the connections between the "facts" of science and the "fictions" of popular entertainment.

The videotape's form is much more simple than that of *Open Night*. In the opening sequence, a TV director, Ian Taylor, is looking at the end of the last episode of a thriller series he's made, with Maurice Burgess and Chris Vine playing a couple of detectives, vaguely reminiscent of the two Ronnies' Piggy Malone and Charley Farley. Taylor thinks he's on to another success, but the Director-General of the BBC (in the form of a huge, black African face that fills a TV screen) tells him that he's got no idea how to tell a story, and sends him down to Schools Television.

In Schools Television, Larraine Hudson and Roger Simcox are making a series about the universe. In each programme, Larraine introduces Simcox, as an Egyptian doctor, or a mediaeval monk, or Copernicus, and Simcox, dead straight, offers varying descriptions of the universe. Simcox suggests that perhaps he should wear "monk's robes or something", but Larraine insists that this is an education programme, "not Morecambe and Wise".

To Simcox's delight, Taylor says he's been sent down to pep the series up a bit, add a bit of sex and violence. Simcox shows Taylor two bits of film about Kepler that he claims to have shot without Larraine's knowledge, in one of which Larraine is burnt as a witch. "Very ingenious," comments Taylor. Then he stumbles on the picture of Kepler's Cosmic

Cup and hits on the idea of re-making *The Maltese Falcon*. He drafts Chris Vine in to play Kepler: Maurice Burgess takes over the Sidney Greenstreet role of the fat man to play Kepler's fellow-astronomer, Tycho de Brahe (discoverer of de Brahe's comet). The rest of the tape shows the re-making of the film. Larraine at first refuses to join in, but by the final sequence she's helping the Bogart figure (who's been taken over by Roger Simcox) to slap the truth out of Kepler.

The story could have turned into little more than an esoteric joke. It didn't, partly because of the seriousness with which we approached the scientific information, and partly because of the care we took in reproducing the details of Huston's movie as accurately as possible, and in capturing the surface style. The performers play all their roles with such total conviction that the video begins to look like a dream, in which everything seems logical and normal, while remaining crazy and strange.

The sequences, for example, in which Roger Simcox offers different models of the universe work precisely because neither they nor the way in which they are presented is being sent up.

Fade in LARRAINE.

LARRAINE. Good evening and welcome to the programme. Tonight in our studio we have an Egyptian doctor who's going to tell us about the universe.

SIMCOX. The universe is a rectangular box. (*Working model appears on screen.*) The earth is the floor. The sky is a cow whose four feet rest on the four corners of the earth. Around the inner walls of the box flows a river, on which the Sun God (*Cartoon image of Sun God.*) and the Moon God (*Cartoon image of Moon God.*) sail their boats. Every month the Moon God is attacked by a ferocious sow and devoured (*Sow devours moon.*) In a fortnight, he is re-born. (*Moon God re-appears.*)

LARRAINE. Thank you very much. (*Fade out.*)

The formula is repeated exactly, as Simcox is introduced as "the monk Macrobius, who's going to tell us about the universe".

SIMCOX. The universe consists of a golden chain. At the base of the chain is the earth, which is subject to decay. Above the earth are the sun and the moon; above the sun and moon the fixed stars; and above the fixed stars the heavens. Above the heavens, the Unmoved Mover, or, as we call him, God. This reflects the social order on earth, where the Pope is above the King, the King above the Barons, the Barons above the serfs, and below the serfs are the worms.

LARRAINE. Thank you very much.

Simcox is introduced as Ptolemy ("The universe is made up of giant wheels"), and then as Copernicus.

SIMCOX. The universe is made up of giant wheels. If, instead of having the earth at the centre of the universe, we put the sun there, or a little to one side, then we need only forty-six wheels instead of Ptolemy's – forty?

These pictures of the universe suddenly become very convincing, because of the seriousness with which they're offered. How could we ever imagine that the planets could go round if they weren't on wheels? In what way is our own view of the universe (gravity? how could anybody believe in that?) more rational and less fanciful?

A similar seriousness is reflected in the approach to *The Maltese Falcon* sequences. The first sequence, for example, is "directed" by Ian Taylor, who instructs the performers (Roger Simcox and Chris Vine) in what they have to do. Simcox walks into Sam Spade's office, with the window that looks out on the neon sign with Spade's name in reverse and

then on to the streets of San Francisco beyond (Chris Vine
had drawn the set from memory in charcoal on a huge piece
of paper). Simcox hangs his hat on a peg that's obviously
simply drawn on the set. The action is performed in such a
matter-of-fact way that an old gag suddenly creates a world
in which hanging hats on drawings of pegs becomes as
reasonable as believing in a universe driven by giant wheels.
It then becomes just as reasonable for Chris Vine (playing
the Peter Lorre part) to enter and announce himself as
Johann Kepler.

Through his direction, Ian Taylor re-creates the scene in
which Peter Lorre holds a gun at Bogart's head and Bogart
disarms Lorre and knocks him out. Following Ian Taylor's
instructions, Simcox and Vine demonstrate precisely what
Bogart and Lorre did in the original movie. In the original,
Bogart searches Lorre to find out who he is. In Ian Taylor's
version, Simcox finds, in Vine's pocket, a folded piece of
paper. He unfolds it – it's a huge sheet and the unfolding
takes a long time. On the sheet there's a diagram – a triangle
fitted perfectly inside a circle: "This, Mr. Spade," Vine tells
him, "was my clue to the mystery of the universe."

In flashback (we used a piece of paper with wavy lines to
fake a 1940's Hollywood fade to flashback) Vine explains,
using paper planets moving round on a blackboard, that
he'd had the idea that the six planets were where they were
in the universe because they fitted together in the way the
five perfect geometrical figures could be fitted together. Vine
becomes lyrical about divine harmony: but then we return
brusquely to the interview in Sam Spade's office. "It didn't
work," says Vine, surprised.

From outside the set, Larraine cuts in. "Of course it
didn't work, because there are nine planets and not six ..."
But Vine continues:

VINE (*as* KEPLER). It didn't work because I was using
two-dimensional figures and the universe is three
dimensional. As soon as I tried it with the five perfect

solids, the planets fitted perfectly. I made a drinking cup
to prove it.

SIMCOX (*as* BOGART). Ah, so that's the drinking cup
you were talking about. (*He holds up an envelope he's
found in* VINE's *pocket.*) Now, tell me. What's in this
envelope?

VINE (*off-handedly*). Oh, it's something I discovered when
I was working on the five perfect solids.

SIMCOX (*reading from paper*). "Planets further away from
the sun move more slowly than those nearer the sun.
People believe that the planets are driven by souls. Either
the souls further away from the sun are lazy, or there is
only one soul, in the sun itself. I prefer to call this soul −
force."

VINE. Can I have my gun back now, Mr. Spade?

SIMCOX (*handing back gun*). Mr. Kepler: do you realise
that the physics of modern astronomy is based on this
law?

VINE. Mr. Spade, you will please stick your hands at the
back of your neck. I intend to search your office.

The handing back of the gun was an exact quotation from
the original movie − but Lorre had been looking for the
Maltese Falcon. Like Lorre, Chris Vine, as Kepler, is totally
obsessed with the object of his imaginings − not so much the
drinking cup itself as the concept of perfect harmony, the
perfect solids fitting together like music to make the perfectly
conceived universe. It was this obsession, according to
Koestler, that drove Kepler on through his laborious seven
year battle with the orbit of Mars, and through the rest of his
life as a scientific philosopher. Yet the dream was no more
than a phantom of his imagination − as Larraine points out,
it was built on a scientific absurdity. But while he was
pursuing the phantom, he stumbled on his three great laws.
In our sequence, the law turns up as a by-product. The

significance of that shift from "soul" to "force" is lost on a
Kepler obsessed with his search for the cup. The Huston
movie had given us an exact, precise image of a complex,
mysterious process of the scientific imagination.

The seriousness with which the performers offer the
world they've created produces a texture in which the
extraordinary is treated in a completely matter-of-fact way.
It becomes completely normal, for example, for Maurice
Burgess (in the Sidney Greenstreet fat man's role) to be
holding forth to Sam Spade, not about the Maltese Falcon,
but about Tycho de Brahe's discovery of a new star.

BURGESS. According to Aristotle, change was limited to
the earth. In the sphere of the fixed stars, nothing ever
changed. Nothing new was possible. Now this is going to
be the most astounding thing you ever heard, sir. Sit
down.

He pours SIMCOX a drink.

BURGESS. On the 11th of November, 1572, I was
walking home to supper when, glancing at the sky, I saw a
star where no star had ever been before. The star was
brighter than Venus at its brightest. The place was a little
to the north-west of Cassiopeia, which then stood near the
zenith. You must know the spot, sir, near the famous W.

SIMCOX. Uh-huh.

BURGESS. Naturally, I couldn't believe my eyes. If this
really was a new star, not only Aristotle, but the whole of
Platonic and Christian doctrine would be shaken. I called
my servants and my peasants to confirm that the star was
really there. But it was there, sir, and remained visible for
eighteen months.

SIMCOX. I guess you could say it was pretty well fixed.

BURGESS. That was the question, sir. Was it a fixed star or
wasn't it? All over Europe stargazers were holding up
pieces of thread to try and measure whether the star was

moving. And this, sir, was my great opportunity. Can you imagine what first attracted me about the stars?

SIMCOX. I guess they were easier on your eyes than the peasants ...

BURGESS. It was the possibility of precise prediction. (BURGESS *has poured* SIMCOX *another drink and as he talks he watches* SIMCOX *very carefully.*) ... The old planetary tables were a month out in their reckoning. I decided to make instruments that could produce more precise measurements. When the new star appeared, I'd just finished my latest instrument. It was a sextant with arms five and a half feet long. I was able to prove that the new star didn't move. And that was the end of Aristotle's chain of being.

SIMCOX *slumps in his chair. His brandy glass falls to the floor.*

In the sequence, we tried once again to capture the rhythms and actions of a scene from the Huston movie – the one between Greenstreet and Bogart in which Greenstreet talks about the bird, while slipping Bogart a drugged drink. But we're taken into a world where Aristotle's chain of being is accepted as being as familiar as the trappings of a gangster movie. It doesn't seem in any way incongruous for Roger Simcox (as Bogart/Sam Spade) to be sitting in Spade's office, reading a newspaper, and suddenly to read aloud an item of news:

On the 13th of October Tycho de Brahe had dinner at the illustrious Rosenberg's table, and held back his water beyond the bounds of courtesy. When he drank more he felt the tension in his bladder increase. When he got home he could scarcely urinate. Internal fevers led to delirium and on the 24th October his delirium ceased and he expired peacefully.

Naturally, he reads the item in his Bogart voice.

Towards the end of Huston's movie, Bogart has the Maltese Falcon delivered to him in the presence of the gang of crooks. But Greenstreet, shaving it with his knife, discovers that it's a fake. "What is it?" somebody asks Bogart, pointing to the bird. And Bogart replies, "The stuff that dreams are made of."

In the closing sequence of our version of the movie, Chris Vine, as Kepler, is waiting for the Cosmic Cup to be delivered ("There's a man outside with a bundle. He seems to be watching the house"). Simcox and Larraine (who's been dragged into the story) interrogate him: "Tell me, what do you know about the secant of the angle of five degrees and eighteen minutes?" Vine uses a soda siphon and two wine glasses to set up a demonstration of orbits: they're drawn in charcoal on the set, but they become real when they're taken down. Once again he becomes lyrical as he describes his scientific discoveries.

VINE. I felt as if I had been awakened from a deep sleep ... Why should I mince my words, Mr. Spade. The truth of nature which I had rejected returned by stealth through the back door. (*He casually hands* SIMCOX *an envelope.*) Oh, what a foolish bird I had been!

SIMCOX (*opens envelope, reads*): Kepler's first and most important law! "All planets move in elliptical orbits." Precious, this opens the way for a modern physics of the sky.

VINE. And now, perhaps, I can have my cosmic cup.

There's heavy music. Everything goes dark. A shaft of light comes through a creaking door. A bundle, wrapped in newspaper, drops on the table. The room lights up again. VINE *begins to unwrap the parcel.*

VINE (*unwrapping*). The Cosmic Cup! The harmony of the universe! The heavenly motions are nothing but a continuous song for several voices!

He finds a tiny piece of paper. He begins to unfold it: it *takes a long time to unfold. When it's finally open we read in huge letters across the paper the formula "$e = mc^2$".*

VINE *stares uncomprehendingly at the paper.*

VINE. What's this, Mr. Spade?

SIMCOX. The stuff that dreams are made of.

The image was intended to demonstrate, succinctly, the way the nightmare world of modern physics had grown out of Kepler's dreams. But we'd found the image in something that was itself a dream — an old, popular and often-televised John Huston movie.

Re-making *The Maltese Falcon* as a video about Johann Kepler was, no doubt, a bizarre activity. It was also peculiarly apt. We worked with obsession on *his* dream of the harmony of the universe.

In working on his obsession, Kepler discovered scientific laws. What had we discovered? Primarily, I think, that the possibilities of video are being wasted if it's thought of simply as a visual aid.

We'd begun working on *Sam Spade Meets Johann Kepler* with the intention of trying to find a way of putting across scientific information in an entertaining, and, therefore, memorable form. But the more we explored the forms we were working with, the less important the putting across of that information became. What came to matter was the way the language of a popular form — the gangster movie — could be used to open up new ways of looking at historical or scientific information.

The project also opened up possible ways of working with films. Instead of seeing *The Maltese Falcon* in terms of film history, or of genre, we saw it as a basis for imaginative work. Through the work we were brought to grips with both film and scientific history.

We showed the completed tape mainly to sixth forms and

general studies groups. In general, they found the tape intriguing. Science students in particular were often anxious to take issue with its implications. They, too, have become familiar with the conventional image of a scientist as a man who is rational, methodical, practical (in contrast to the "artist", whom they think of as irrational and emotional). To be presented with a scientist making important discoveries while chasing a phantom is to have that conventional image challenged.

I don't know how much viewers in the end learnt about Kepler and his scientific discoveries: it seemed to me that if people *wanted* to learn about those things they already had material available in books, and that, in thinking about using television for educational purposes, it was important to ask what the medium could do that books couldn't. Koestler had been able to describe Kepler's thought processes: but it needed video to create that particular concrete image of a Peter Lorre Kepler passionately searching for his Cosmic Cup.

In an epilogue to the videotape, we added our own comment on the usefulness or otherwise of "educational television" as a visual aid. As the final image of *The Cosmic Cup* rolls on the screen, the group involved in making the video are seen sitting round the monitor. "This is the way to make educational programmes!" says Simcox. "We could do a musical version of the quantum theory." Ian Taylor sings, "Einstein, Einstein, measuring the universe ...".

But Paul Kerrigan, the student who's been handling the sound, suddenly takes off his earphones.

"What does it mean − E equals MC two?" he asks.

The videotape has failed to explain.

But in terms of offering a learning experience, that didn't seem to me to matter at all.

Project Three: Spies at Work

Open Night and *Sam Spade Meets Johann Kepler* had been planned as video projects to follow up the theatre work of the Bradford Art College Theatre Group.

Spies at Work, on the other hand, grew out of a number of video projects we'd tried with groups of Bradford school-leavers. In the other two projects, we'd used the language of popular TV entertainment to question assumptions about both the TV and education services we've got. In *Spies at Work* we offered young people the chance of making their own video entertainment.

We'd invited groups of 12–15 pupils out of school for one week at a time to work with us on the video. We'd offered the projects around the Bradford schools, stipulating, first, that we wouldn't take more than four pupils in any one group from any one school (so that they would have to work with other pupils they'd never worked with before) and, secondly, that only pupils who *wanted* to come and work on the projects and who'd positively chosen to do so should be accepted. (In practice, though, we found that some teachers were only too glad to get rid of *their* unteachables.)

We began by playing and inventing video games with the groups. But at some point in every project the young people always wanted to use the video to tell stories. The stories tended to be limited in scope. A typical story, *Smash and Grab*, showed a girl making a date with her boyfriend to go to the pictures. When she leaves her boy-friend, two other boys follow her and attack her. They try to snatch her handbag, but she bashes them with it. Then her boy-friend arrives, like the US cavalry, and puts the marauders to flight.

Another story showed two boys picking up two girls in a cinema. It contains a classic invitation to romance: "D'you fancy goin' to't fish an' chip shop after?" When one of the boys, gallantly but clumsily tries to help a girl on with her coat, she says, "It 'as got sleeves, yer know."

The stories were free and relaxed and entertaining. But

one reason why they were so limited in subject matter was that it never occurred to the school-leavers that they were free to try something more ambitious. And this was why I suggested trying to work in a specific *genre* – and making a spy story.

The aim was, in fact, for three different groups to work on the same videotape. The first group would kick the story off, working for the first week; the second group would work for a second week developing the story; and the third group would use the final week to provide an ending. We'd put all the three weeks' work together and show all three groups the finished tape.

At one stage we planned to use portapak, and turn Bradford into Berlin, finding images of East and West Berlin and of the Wall in areas of the city. But the portapak broke down on the first day – so we took our studio in what had once been The Vaults bar and turned that into Berlin instead.

If we were to make a videotape with three different groups of school-leavers in three weeks, we needed to develop very quickly a way of working. From the start we decided to avoid editing. We began each sequence by fading in, and ended each sequence by fading out, so that it became a simple matter to re-record the sequences one after the other on to a master-tape. The repeated device of fading in and fading out gave the videotape a particular rhythm. The fades created a kind of punctuation.

The device meant that each sequence had to be prepared, rehearsed and recorded in a block. To make the blocks as long and continuous as possible, we had to work out how to change the position of one camera while continuing to record on another (we used three cameras in all). Rehearsing didn't simply mean rehearsing the performers. It meant everybody – performers, camera-people, switcher, sound-recorder – all practising a sequence together, as if they were a football team working at a set-piece. We didn't script each sequence before shooting. We started each sequence from scratch, worked out physically what was going to happen both to performers and to cameras, did a few dry runs, then tried out a recording. When we'd got a version we liked, we scripted it up from the recording, words, actions, camera-movements, switching cues, the lot. Only the switcher used the script – the rest kept all their moves for each sequence in their heads. When we were satisfied with a sequence, we kept it on tape and moved on to the next.

This way of working was, I believe, important for school-leavers who weren't used to handling words and concepts in the abstract. Some years later, I was to read of an "A" level course in Communications in which students were allowed to enter videotapes instead of essays. But in order to qualify for the right to use the equipment, a student was required to offer "i) a definition of the target audience; ii) a modified story board, showing key points and sequences with details of music and sound effects; iii) photographs of visual material (captions, slides, film sequences) prepared according to a standard format; iv) script, giving full instructions for production crew without the need for any additional instructions".

Such requirements take video – which, to me, is valuable precisely *because* it offers a non-literary way of creating – back into a safe academic prison. If we'd asked for requirements like this, the school-leavers who invented *Spies at Work* would have been cut off from video as they'd been cut off from most other academic subjects.

We couldn't have offered a script prepared in advance, because when we began we had no idea what the story would be about. We showed the first group a spy film set in Berlin. It contained a sequence in which someone has to pass on a telephone number to someone else. The number is written on the bottom of a coffee cup.

After they'd seen the film, the group decided to invent ways of passing on messages. They divided into pairs, worked for a while, and then came back with ideas. The first recordings were all about *how* messages could be passed on.

After a time, it became necessary to decide what the message was. So everybody wrote a message on a piece of paper. The pieces of paper were put into a hat. One boy had by this time become a newspaper seller. He would stand with a bundle of newspapers under his arm beside a placard which read, SPY QUESTION IN HOUSE. He picked a message out of the hat and tucked the message at random into one of his newspapers. The rest of the performers then queued up to buy newspapers. And the one who got the newspaper with the message inside was responsible for setting up the next scene.

A girl got the newspaper with the message. She read the message, but kept the contents to herself. At that point she became the only person in the room who knew what the story was about, and she became automatically the director of the next sequence.

Working in this way, the group invented the story as the first week went on. By the Thursday lunch-time, after three and a half days' work, we had rough versions of enough sequences to make thirteen minutes of story. We spent the last day and a half working from these rough versions to produce a finished recording of the sequences in order.

By that time, the group had formed itself naturally into a team. Some liked performing, some liked to handle the cameras, one girl put herself in charge of the mixer. But earlier in the week, they'd all had a go at everything.

During that first week, in particular, the group very quickly mastered what used to be called "the grammar of the film", the art of telling a story in pictures. They invented sequences in which the story had to be passed from one camera to another. For example: a boy sits at a table in a street café, orders a beer and takes off his hat. He works his hat to the edge of the table and, as if accidentally, a scrap of paper falls from under the hat to the floor. There's a close-up of the scrap of paper, then a shot of a brush sweeping it away. We follow the boy who's doing the brushing and then see another close-up of the brush sweeping the scrap of paper under a newspaperman's placard. Then there's a shot of the newspaperman. Very casually, he bends down and picks up the scrap of paper. As he's reading it, a man with dark glasses moves into shot, and leans on the placard. The newspaperman hurriedly puts the scrap of paper away. (It was all taken in one continuous sequence, and involved at least eight camera changes.)

The group used the language of popular cinema with complete naturalness. There's one moment, for example, where the whole gang is sitting round a table being addressed by their leader (the girl who'd found the message in the newspaper). "We got the wrong man," she says. Two of the gang are wearing black bowlers. Without saying a word, they very reverently take them off together.

Nearly the whole of that first week's work was shot in front of a blank white sheet – with the result that the movements take on a quality of abstraction. For example, a bench is seen in front of the white background. A boy walks on, wearing a long coat and a black bowler. He sits on the bench, takes off the bowler and places it on the seat beside him. He takes out a newspaper and reads.

Another boy arrives. He's also wearing a long coat and a black bowler. He, too, sits on the bench, takes off the bowler and places it on the seat beside him. And he, too, takes out a newspaper and reads.

Presently, the second boy folds up his newspaper, puts it away, picks up the wrong bowler, puts it on his head, stands up and walks out of shot. The first boy cautiously feels under the hat the other one has left. He finds a scrap of screwed-up paper, opens it, reads it. A boy with dark glasses comes and sits beside him on the bench. The first boy hurriedly hides the paper, puts on his hat, stands up and walks away.

The two boys had originally imagined the scene taking place in a park. But there's no attempt to create the park: you can hear the sound of footsteps on a wooden floor and there's no attempt to disguise the sound. All the emphasis is on the abstracts of passing the message.

There's no attempt either to disguise the fact that these are sixteen-year-old boys *pretending* to be Hollywood spies. But the sequence works because of the seriousness with which it's played. When the two boys had first invented the scene, they'd played it very quickly. But as they worked on it, played it back, studied what they'd done, they found that they could play the actions very slowly and deliberately. (One vital factor about working with video, as distinct from film, is that students can see themselves immediately on screen. The work becomes *real*.)

We discovered, too, that the story could be told through a series of extremely simple, but highly visual images. The boy with dark glasses, simply walking into a shot and standing there, became a repeated image of threat. A cripple, on crutches, selling matches, hobbling slowly across the screen at the end of each sequence became a mysterious figure in the story.

In the final tape, these images create a slow, measured rhythm. Out of this slowness, action suddenly leaps, very quick and direct. The cripple is leaning against a wall. He begins to hobble slowly forward. The boy who's sweeping the floor uses his broom to knock a crutch from under the cripple. The cripple falls. The boy with the broom quickly searches the cripple, finds an identity card, looks at it, holds up his thumb. Another boy, who's leaning against the wall reading a newspaper, takes out a gun, holds it with two hands, Starsky and Hutch style, and fires repeated shots at the cripple. There's the sound of real shots on the sound-track, and this suddenly calls attention to the abstracts of the killing itself. There's no conventional "dramatic" build-up: only a sudden violence.

There's a similar eruption later when the gang confront their boss around a table. (The boss is the girl who found the message in the newspaper and became the director of the scene.) She makes no attempt to disguise the fact that she's a school-girl, wears a wide skirt just below the knee and heavy box shoes. But she sits swigging brandy, which she pours herself from a bottle, Hollywood gang-boss style.

The dialogue is laconic: we invented the lines sitting around the table for ten minutes before the recording took place – each character selected one line and kept to it.

GIRL (*throws identity card on table*). We got the wrong man. (*Two spies take off their hats. The* GIRL *questions the spies one by one.*) What have you got to say for yourself?

FIRST SPY. I wasn't even there.

GIRL. Well, what are you doing here now? Get out. (SPY *leaves.* GIRL *looks at* NEWSPAPERMAN.) What about you?

NEWSPAPERMAN. All I were doing was selling papers.

GIRL. Well, get back to selling them. (MAN *leaves with papers and placard.* GIRL *turns to* SPY *with gun.*) Why did you shoot him?

SECOND SPY (*indicating man with broom*). He told me to.

GIRL. You know what to do, don't you?

The assassin pulls out his gun and shoots the boy with the broom. The action is once again quick, sudden, direct, and there are again real gunshots on the soundtrack. The boy with the broom falls behind the table, directly, without any fuss. His broom clatters after him. The action is sharp and clear. It's as if they were *demonstrating* killing, as a casual, matter-of-fact operation, rather than performing "drama".

Towards the end of the week the group discovered that, even without a portapak, they weren't tied to the Vaults Bar. They could record exterior sequences by shooting through a corner window. So the climax of their episode took place at the bottom of Bradford's Great Horton Road, with coffee bars and newsagents to the left, the crazy domes of the Alhambra Theatre to the right, cars parked on both sides of the street, a busy dual carriageway full of cars and pedestrians at the bottom of a hill, and, in the background, beyond the new glass-house police station, the Florentine tower of the old Bradford City Hall. It was a rich, seedily eccentric location, which was suddenly peopled by characters from *Spies at Work*.

As the sequence appears in the final tape, a boy in a long coat and wearing a black bowler comes into shot, walking down the street. The camera follows him as he walks past a newspaperman, selling newspapers in an alley opposite the Vaults Bar, and standing beside a placard that reads, SPY QUESTION IN HOUSE. The boy who's walking down the street is nervous: he keeps glancing over his shoulder. Suddenly, we're aware that he's being followed by a small, wiry figure wearing a cowboy hat: we see the two of them in long-shot. The first boy begins to run down the middle of the street. So does the second. The first boy loses his bowler, which drops in the road, just as a sinister-looking black car, which has been turning in the cul-de-sac at the bottom of the street, comes back up the hill towards the camera. The car runs over the bowler, and when the car has gone, so has the bowler. (The whole business with the car and the hat happened completely by accident: it looks like a very effective piece of planning.)

The two boys run on. When the first, in the long coat, reaches the pavement by the dual-carriageway, the one with the cowboy hat stops, pulls out a gun, kneels, takes careful aim and, using both hands, fires. The boy with the long coat flings both his arms high in the air, and topples forward, over the top of a huge litter bin, and out of sight on to the pavement. Pedestrians and cars pass by, paying no attention.

The camera follows the assassin back up the street. In passing, we see the newspaperman lying dead in the alley, with his placard overturned and his newspapers scattered on the pavement.

A cripple hobbles down the street on crutches.

The sequence was shot entirely without sound, and, again, the killing had a precise, demonstrative quality. All of it looked as if it had happened in a very clear dream. The fact that the passers-by paid no attention turned it, on one level, into the kind of street-game (like Cowboys and Indians) where children fire bullets at each other and adults walk through the line of fire unscathed. And in one sense it *was* a game: the school-leavers were playing at making a movie, built round popular images with which they were as familiar as we were. But they were playing in earnest. What was remarkable was the concentration and commitment and seriousness the young people brought to the work. The seriousness is there on the screen, in a story they know is wryly funny.

INVESTIGATOR. Did you get them all, then?

GIRL. Uh-huh.

INVESTIGATOR. The man with the hat? (GIRL *nods.*)
    The newspaper-seller?

GIRL. Uh-huh.

INVESTIGATOR. The man with the broom?

GIRL. Uh-huh.

INVESTIGATOR. What about the cripple?

GIRL (*after a fractional pause*). We got the wrong one.

INVESTIGATOR. You killed off all your own agents and
    missed the enemy spy?

GIRL. It wasn't my fault.

She's led off at gun-point by the boy in the cowboy hat. The boy with dark glasses enters and leans against a wall.

The seriousness depended primarily on the presence of the video equipment and the fact that the school-leavers were themselves put in control of it.

TV is a familiar and real element in everybody's lives – unlike theatre, which belongs only to the few. When you can look at a TV monitor and see, there on the screen, images that you yourself have made, and can see yourself performing, the experience of doing imaginative work also becomes real. What you've imagined and what you've performed are there, frozen on tape, imagination made concrete.

The boy who played the newspaperman responded to the video in a way he could never have responded to a theatre workshop. He was sixteen years old, but he was very tall and mature and looked much older. In the three previous years, we were told, he'd spent only a few weeks in school. But he never missed a session of the video project and insisted on coming back for the second and third weeks.

In the second and third weeks, though, we ran into problems. The same degree of concentration wasn't achieved again, largely because, as the story developed, the possibilities of invention were narrowed down. The first group had total freedom of invention: whereas the work of the later groups was already to some extent limited by the images created in that first week. The second and third groups were never able to make the work their own.

Where the other groups did get involved was in sequences in which they were themselves discovering new possibilities.

The group in the second week, for example, used what was in the Vaults Bar to create outdoor scenes indoors. A group of art students had made a two-dimensional cut-out railway carriage, life-size, for an exhibition they'd been involved in the previous term. The school-leavers used this train. They fed into the sound system the noise of a train coming into a station and creaking to a stop. As the sequence faded in, the train was already there, obviously held up by the passengers sitting inside it. It jerked convincingly in time to the noises on the soundtrack.

Later the same group created a football match. Eight of them stood, crowded together on the screen waving scarves and shouting, with crowd noises in the background. The story was carried forward by two of them talking together in close-up, each plot point being punctuated by roars from the crowd. The sequence ended with what was obviously a goal, and with all of them jumping wildly up and down.

There was also a very atmospheric scene in the country. Two Christmas trees were held to look like bushes at the entrance to a tunnel. Boys in greatcoats stood by the trees, beating their arms and stamping their feet in the cold. It looked dark and there was silence. Suddenly, there was a whistle; running feet; a police siren; and the sound of machine-gun fire as a body was hurried into the tunnel ...

The third group found a way of shooting a sequence outside in the street, through the window, and dubbing on the dialogue in the studio afterwards. The scene took place in front of the dark walls of the public baths across the road. Two girls were waiting. A boy came running out of the alley down the street, ran up to them and gave them a brief-case. There was a hurried dialogue. The group invented the dialogue before they recorded the outdoor scene. Then they recorded the scene, speaking to each other the lines they'd invented. Finally they came back into the Vaults Bar and, stop-watch in hand, synchronised the dialogue with the pictures on the screen.

The last shot of all should have been easy. A wounded man is seen crawling along the ground. Cut to a close-up of the Berlin Wall (in fact, a section of the old brick fireplace in the Vaults Bar). Black-gloved hands are feeling their way up the wall. One hand finds the top and holds it, while the other gropes its way up. Then the two hands hold what's obviously the weight of the wounded man, hanging from the top of the Berlin Wall. There's the sound of a machine-gun. The two hands slide down the wall.

The boy who played the part was very tall. He could reach the top of the fireplace easily. He didn't look as if he were hanging from the wall. A smaller boy showed him how to do it. We got him to look at the way hands contracted when they held a body. But still the tall boy couldn't make it look right. Finally, we got the tall boy to kneel down and pull himself up from a kneeling position, and the shot worked.

The most satisfying moment in the last week's work came when two teachers arrived one afternoon to see how their pupils were getting on. A girl was on the point of giving a police briefing, using a crude map of the Berlin Wall that had been drawn on the blackboard. The teachers were asked to sit down in the police class. And the girl gave them a chalk and talk lesson about what was going on.

The World Premiere of *Spies at Work* took place one afternoon a few weeks later in the room where the videotape had been made. We'd invited all the pupils who'd worked on the video – it was the first time that the groups had come together. And we'd invited their teachers, and the press, and anybody else who might be interested. By sheer chance, a free-lance journalist, who wrote for the highly technical magazine, *Video*, happened to be in college that day. A few weeks later the faces of thirty Bradford school-leavers gazed out from the front cover at video enthusiasts all over the country.

We staged the afternoon with care, giving flowers to the performers, interviewing them (on video) as they arrived. Everybody got a *Spies at Work* identity card, which we'd designed and printed as a souvenir. The viewing of the work itself became a celebratory event.

What had they learned?

They certainly hadn't learned anything about the political and economic problems which had led to the building of the Berlin Wall – a "liberal studies" topic I'd had in mind at the beginning of the project.

But they had learned how to work the video; how to invent a collective story; how to tell that story in pictures; how to use popular TV and movie images.

They'd also learned that learning itself can be enjoyable,

and that it needn't depend on people in authority. Different people had taken over the direction at different times. We hadn't offered any solutions: some of them had turned out to be more technically inventive than we were.

At the same time, though, they'd learned that at particular moments *somebody* needed to take decisions if the work was to go forward. They accepted, for example, the decisions of the girl who found the message hidden in the newspaper. The videotape wasn't made by committee, but by collective agreement. They'd learned that in order to achieve a result, they needed discipline. But not a discipline imposed by an outside authority: their discipline was self-generated.

They'd learned that the school situation — in which other people devise timetables, say what you should learn, when, and for how long — isn't the only one in which work is possible: that, in fact, it's an abnormal way of working, and that work can generate its own momentum.

Above all, they'd learned that their ideas and suggestions would be taken seriously, would actually be listened to because they were needed. Most of them had been labelled academic failures. They'd been taught by experience that they didn't belong to the elite that mattered, the nineteen per cent who would go on to reap the career, status and economic rewards of higher education. They hadn't made it, and, for several years, they hadn't been expected to make it. They'd been labelled and been taught to accept the labelling: and so they'd decided that education wasn't for them.

Suddenly, people were looking with interest at their work, and enjoying it. The screen images briefly gave them back their own validity.

Spies at Work was never intended to be about the problem of being a school-leaver in Bradford. But when the finished videotape was taken around the schools where they'd been pupils, the screenings affected the way the schools saw them. Teachers who'd come to expect nothing from them looked at them, momentarily, with a surprised respect.

Momentarily, because there were no resources to follow up the work begun in *Spies at Work*. Within a few months, most of the group were on the dole. It would have been logical to set up a film and video studio and pay them a basic grant to do more work. Instead, a working party was set up to examine what could be done for unemployed young people in Bradford. The working party recommended that a technical course should be set up to train young people for "practical" jobs. None of the group who worked on *Spies at Work* joined the technical course.

One of them did work briefly on *Sam Spade Meets Johann Kepler*, before becoming a waiter. Another worked on a film financed by the National Film School with a group of young West Indians in Bradford, called *Black Future*. We tried to get him a grant to survive – but he was persuaded to join the Navy before the grant came through.

In the education system we've got, non-academic 16-year-old school-leavers aren't assumed to be capable of helping to extend research. Their place is on the shop floor, or in the dole queue – or helping to defend the society we've got. Which is the society that's labelled them failures in the first place.

PART THREE

Towards a Popular Education

When we began work on the video projects, our aim was to offer a contribution to a discussion about the possible uses of popular entertainment forms by those involved in educational television. But as we developed the work, it seemed to me that the ideas and methods we were exploring were relevant, not simply to the television industry, but to anybody who believes in the urgent need to create new forms of popular education.

The work points in two main directions: first, towards the possible uses of video games: and, secondly towards the uses of the language of popular entertainment.

In both cases, the work is based on the assumption that a group of people have come together to do something they *want* to do. To impose video as one more school subject would be to bring a potentially popular form into the authority-imposed structure of the education we've got.

The idea of video games was an extension of work in theatre games, which had, in turn, grown out of methods developed by Joan Littlewood and Clive Barker in Theatre Workshop.

We'd used the theatre games as a way of destroying conventional educational hierarchies. We'd invented situations in which young people who'd been labelled as failures at school could *win*. For example, one week of

theatre games, played with Bradford school-leavers, had led
to the performance of a version of *Ars Longa*, *Vita Brevis*,
by John Arden and Margaretta D'Arcy, in which the
school-leavers played at being their own teachers. They
performed the version to a group of teacher training
students, who were studying Arden in "Drama".
Afterwards, a perky little boy said to the future teachers, "If
there's anything you didn't understand, don't be frightened
to put your hands up and ask questions."

The video games had the advantage over the theatre
games of being involved with images on a television screen.
The "theatre" was remote from the lives of most of the
young people we worked with. Television was, on the other
hand, taken for granted. Being able to see themselves on the
screen, and to use the hardware, made the work that much
more real and that much more adult.

From the start we concentrated on making the equipment
an integral part of the game. We weren't primarily interested
in using the cameras simply to *record* theatre games. When
we played video "hide the thimble" the camera was itself
the seeking eye: the recorded images were there as part of
the search.

Another game developed spontaneously when a girl
pretended to use a camera as if it were a maching-gun. We
took a shot of her using her camera to execute three blind-
folded figures who were standing against the wall – then we
cut to her camera which was leaping wildly up and down.
Her camera recorded a grotesque, wildly jumping image of
people dying in strange poses. The camera was not just a
recording device: it was part of the scene.

The equipment was also an integral part of the random-
cutting game. The person who controlled the mixer sat there
turning up playing cards and used the mixer to cut from one
camera to another every time a picture card was turned up.
The two players sitting in front of the two cameras were only
allowed to speak when their particular camera was switched
on. The players were holding a dialogue with each other: but

they were staring at and talking to the camera. To emphasise the direct relationship of talking head to camera, we set the heads against a blank white background, with nothing to distract from the face and the words.

When we adapted a game of "Murder" for video, the recorded image on the monitor became an essential element in the game. Three or four people created the image: the rest of the group had to scrutinise the image to discover a murderer.

"Murder" is best played by three performers in front of three cameras who record a piece of video. One of the three performers is assumed to be guilty of murder.

The performers sit, one in front of each camera. Each is required to talk when the light on the camera indicates that his (or her) camera is on. As in the other random-cutting games, the person working the mixer switches from one camera to another at the dictation of a pack of face-down playing cards, which he turns up one by one, switching whenever he turns up a picture card.

Each of the three performers has to invent and stick to an alibi. When the light on your camera is switched on, you start describing your alibi and keep on talking until the light goes out. When the light comes on again, you continue with your story. So that, in effect, on the tape, there are three stories being told – all of them constantly interrupted by the random cutting.

There is, however, yet another rule which the performers have to remember. For the clue to the identity of the murderer is (in the simplest version of the game) a visual and not a verbal clue. For example: two of the story-tellers sit throughout with their arms folded, the third keeps touching his (or her) hair, nervously. The guilty person is the one who touches the hair. (Naturally, the group who's trying to guess the murderer doesn't know this. Normally, the people in the group begin by studying the *stories* very carefully).

The performers, therefore, don't have to worry overmuch about what they actually say. They have to worry about being ready to talk when their cameras come on, and about making sure they keep to the correct poses or gestures. And precisely because they're not worrying about whether or not their stories and language are "correct", they're made free to use words as they come. Faced with an examination question, "You are accused of committing a murder. Write down your alibi", they would be struggling to find words. (It would be an unusually imaginative O level question anyway.) Faced with cameras switched on at random, the stories flow:

> Well, there I was, having my bath. I've run the water nearly to the top, and I've got all this pink, bubbly stuff all covering my knees, and there's this knock at the door, and when I get to the door there's this copper, and he says, you know that old woman next door, well, she'd been murdered, and we think you might know summat about it. Me? I said. Why me? I mean, I know she were a miserable old bugger, I wouldn't have minded murdering her if I'd thought of it, but, I mean to say, do I *look* like I'd go round murdering people. I don't go round murdering people. I mean, I'm a right nice kind person ...

The "Murder" game illustrates one of the main uses of the video games – making it possible for players to use their own language. Both television and the schools teach that there are correct ways of using language if you wish to be taken "seriously" either on the screen or in the examination room. The BBC announcer, Sue Lawley, has said that she had to lose her Birmingham accent in order to become a presenter of the magazine programme, *Nationwide*. O level passages for "comprehension" offer examples of what officialdom regards as acceptable language:

> The southernmost area of South America, from Cape Horn to the northern shore of the Magellan Strait is one of the least known, the most hostile and yet most beautiful areas in the world.

It's in this kind of language that pupils know they're supposed to write about such topics as "The Art of Choosing and Wearing Clothes", or "Do you consider that we live in a violent age?" ("Should hanging be brought back?" two 13-year-old schoolboys had been asked, by their teacher, to discuss in front of our video cameras. They thought it was not necessary, "in this day and age".)

Confronted with the need to use a language that's alien to them, working-class young people often freeze up — as a result of which they're categorised as "non-verbal". With at least some of them the "Murder" game had had the effect of unfreezing.

As well as encouraging people to use their own language, the "Murder" game offers scope for inventiveness. The first time people play the game, those "investigating" the murder don't know they're looking for a visual clue: they study the words, until one of them spots the gesture. So the gesture can at first be simple — the guilty person touching his hair. But once groups know that they're looking for visual clues, the performers have to invent increasingly complicated gestures to fool the investigators. Instead of two performers sitting with arms folded, while the third one touches his hair, they all need to have gestures of some kind. A group of three 16-year-old girls in Bradford spent a whole morning developing extremely complicated routines, while still telling their stories. Eventually they ended up gesturing like RADA actresses in an audition — only two of them gestured with both hands, very dramatically, while the third, the guilty one, gestured with only one hand. Finally, they produced another tape in which all three of them gestured with both hands. Nobody could spot the murderer, and some of us studied it for days before we realised that two of the three girls were beginning every bit of story with the word, "Well …". They'd switched back to a verbal clue, and were delighted that we'd found it so hard to spot.

Observation is another skill that's encouraged by the "Murder" game. The group that's trying to spot the clue is forced to scrutinise the tape again and again: they find themselves looking at a television screen in a much more concentrated way than they normally would. And they analyse what they see, not because they're asked to do an exercise in "television analysis", but because analysis is part of the game.

"Murder" can be played with only two cameras and four performers. In fact, all the random cutting games can become team activities. Two chairs are placed, one in front of each camera. The two teams line up beside the two chairs. The two players at the head of the lines sit, one in each chair. When the first camera is switched on, the first player starts talking. Then, when there's a cut to the second camera, and while the second player is talking, the first player has to get quickly out of his or her chair, and the next player in the line tries to get into position on the chair to be ready to talk as soon as the camera is switched on again. This version of the game becomes physical, with players from both teams rushing in and out of the chairs. The aim is to keep one dialogue going, as if there were only two players. The physical action helps to reduce even further the players' self-consciousness about using words, and even in the rough-and-tumble it's necessary to concentrate, because you've got to listen all the time to the way the conversation is going.

In yet another version of this game, one player in one chair plays against a team of players who line up beside the other chair. A topic we found useful in this version was a request for higher wages. The single person played the boss, the rest of the group played workers asking for a wage demand.

We usually leave the players themselves free to choose the content of the conversation, making suggestions only if they can't think of anything. (One interesting fact we discovered was that university students, teacher training students and teachers themselves had much more difficulty with the content than the school-leavers. The school-leavers tended to talk quite directly about experiences they were familiar with — asking mam if the dinner was ready, arguing about why somebody was late for a date — whereas the university students invariably felt that they had to be clever and funny: "I ask myself — was Marx a Marxist?", and so on.)

It is possible, though, to use the random cutting for specific purposes. While inventing a show about Australian Rules Football with a group of drama students in Melbourne, we played at footballers being called before a disciplinary tribunal. With another group who were studying "community theatre", we played a version in which the group had to explain to Goebbels why they wanted a grant to do community theatre in Nazi Germany. ("We want to strengthen people's sense of community" and "We want to make them more aware of threats to moral and spiritual values" were O.K. statements — "We want to use theatre to help people control and change their society" wasn't.)

We used the *Colditz/School* game I've described to invent dialogue and characters for *Open Night*. "Pull yourself together, Simcox. Remember who you are" led to one of the repeated gags in *Open Night*, "The name's Forster, sir." "Ah, yes, Forster, Simcox".

The random cutting game could, in fact, be very useful to drama groups trying to create a collective script through improvisation. The pressure of trying to push on a story while playing the game leads to surprising verbal inventions, which are then there, on tape, to be used. In the *Colditz/School* tape, Knowles was describing to Simcox how the camp guard nipped over the wire and went to the village pub. "He goes to the village pub and he gets pobbled," said Knowles under the pressure of the game. Simcox's eyes lit up at the new word. "He gets what?" he said, trying to keep a straight face. "He gets pobbled?" The camera cut back to Knowles, who, by this time, had realised he'd invented a new word. Knowles went on, with great assurance, "Yes, he gets pobbled, and he buys chocolate and cigarettes and brings them back to sell on the black market …".

The *Coldtiz/School* tape was useful in developing material. It was also, at times, entertaining in its own right.

Another game which directly involves the camera as an active element is one which we called the *Slave/Teacher* game. The game needs two fixed cameras. One is fixed on two "actors" who are rehearsing a very short scene. The other is fixed on the "teacher", who is sitting at the mixer, directing the scene. Because the "teacher" handles the mixer, he (or she) is always in total control of what is recorded on the screen — he can cut from the "actors" to put a picture of himself on the screen any time he likes.

The "actors" begin rehearsing. When the "teacher" has had enough, he presses the switch and puts himself on the screen. As soon as the "teacher" appears on the screen, the "actors" stop rehearsing, while the teacher gives directions: "Try it a bit faster. Can you put a little more emotion into that bit ...?" When the teacher cuts back to the picture of the "actors" they continue the rehearsal.

But there's one more element. When the "teacher" presses the switch to put himself on screen, he either says, "Listen", or "Wait". If he says, "Listen", he keeps himself on screen and gives directions. But if he says, "Wait", he presses the switch and cuts back to the "actors". The "actors" are then free to improvise any conversation they like until the "teacher" puts himself back on screen, and says, "Carry on", after which they go back to the rehearsal.

When we first invented the game in Bradford, we were developing a project called "the school-leavers of Bradford perform the History of the Slave Trade ...". The "teacher" was totally committed to presenting a radical view of history. She talked earnestly to the "school-leavers" about how slavery involved masters controlling slaves, and how everybody should be free and equal. Then she asked them to rehearse a scene showing how a master controlled a slave —

but the game demonstrated that in the process of making the scene she was completely controlling them.

The dialogue that was to be rehearsed was deliberately stylised. A ship's captain is ordering a slave girl to dance: "Dance!" "Never!" "I command you to dance." "I am betrothed to a man and I promised never to dance before anyone but him." "Dance or die!"

When the "teacher" said, "Wait ...", though, the "actors" were free to use their own language. "Now what the bloody hell is she on about?" "I thought I did that bit O.K. Didn't you?" "She doesn't know what she's talking about." "Did you go t'match last Sat'dy?"

The deliberate phoneyness of the dialogue contrasted directly with the naturalness of the language the "school-leavers" used when they were improvising. And the "school-leavers" also played against the "teacher" by deliberately misunderstanding her orders, exaggerating their efforts to obey her, consciously making mistakes. The game became an exercise in passive resistance.

When playing with real school-leavers, we always set it up as a teacher/pupil game. But it can be used to explore any hierarchical situation. With drama students in Melbourne, an Australian colleague (Roberta Bonnin) and I set up a version in which two girls were supposedly creating a play about Women's Liberation. The director was a man, who was giving orders: "For God's sake, remember you're supposed to be *liberated*. Show us your liberation." The session turned into high comedy when something went wrong with the mixer, and the director couldn't get anything but himself on screen. All the men in the room instinctively drifted over to the mixer and began pushing buttons and poking at it. On the screen was the image of men impotently trying to mend a machine.

The game is essentially about ways of coping with authority. But it also demonstrates, very entertainingly, the difference between an imposed language and a language that belongs to the people who speak it.

A number of games we developed were quite simply devised to help people who had difficulty in reading to recognise letters. The simplest involved giving the mixer in the random cutting game a pack of lexicon letter cards instead of playing cards. The mixer was to cut from one camera to the other every time a vowel was turned up.

More imaginative is a game involving three cameras, one, preferably, hidden behind a screen. During the game, groups of letters (e.g. "oi") are advertised.

The person who is learning to recognise letters is behind the screen with a camera fixed on the letters "oi" (we used Scrabble letters). All around are other Scrabble letters. One of the cameras in front of the screen is also fixed on the letters "oi". The third camera is fixed on a person. The person at the mixer watches all three monitors and chooses when to move from one camera to the next.

The game begins with a person on the monitor. The person's job is to advertise a word that includes the letters "oi". For example, the person says: "Does your bicycle have a squeaky chain? Why not use the letters "oi" and …" (at this point the letters "oi" are flashed on and off the screen) "*oi*l it, *oi*l it, *oi*l it …". The person with the Scrabble letter is meanwhile searching for the "l" to complete the word in front of his or her camera. When the person completes the word, it's put on the monitor. Another player might then continue: "Do you want to make tea? Why not put water in a kettle, then use the letters 'oi' and boil it, boil it, boil it." The game continues as long as the players continue to invent ways of using the letters "oi".

The game proved to be very enjoyable, even to people skilled with letters. And it took a lot of the tension out of the simple task of learning to recognise letters – the tension was transferred to the business of playing the game.

But to me it was less important ultimately than the other games which encouraged people to trust their own ability to use language.

Once, when we were working with a group of women on

a Bradford council house estate to produce a news-sheet, we recorded them on sound tape talking about the condition of their own houses. When we transcribed the recordings and printed them in the news-sheet, one of the women looked at the printed transcription with delight and said, "Did I really say that?"

The video games can enable so-called "non-verbal" pupils to *see* themselves talking. The letters game can build up people's confidence in their ability to handle letters – but if I were trying to explore in depth how video could be used to help literacy, I'd want to start with what people themselves say when the games make them feel free to say what they like.

As well as developing and using video games in our work, we were also concerned with finding ways of using the common language of popular television as an educational weapon.

The emphasis was on *using* the language. We were aware of the dangers of turning a popular entertainment form into one more school subject. We were suspicious of the educational trends which were to lead to the establishment of an A level paper in "Communications" in 1978, and of the formation of courses in "mixed ability media studies" – like the one described in *The Times Educational Supplement* (January 1980), in which pupils study comics "with the aid of a recent EAV film strip, *Comics and Cultural History*", make "a close critical study" of *Top of the Pops* on video, and learn to "evaluate" different forms of TV comedy (such as *My Wife Next Door* and *Monty Python*). In the context of popular entertainment, "evaluation" seemed to us a matter of investing our own personal preferences with some kind of spurious academic authority. If we made a "close study" of any individual programme (such as *The Maltese Falcon*), it was because we were in search of ideas and images and ways of putting them together.

So instead of studying the *News*, as the Glasgow University Research Unit which produced *Bad News* did, analysing every item presented over a long period of time, we played with the *News*.

School-leavers made their own *News*. A girl sat in front of a camera, imitated Angela Rippon, and announced: "There have been no sitings of UFO's over Britain for the last six weeks. This is because of the steel strike." The normal logic of the *News* became questionable.

Another girl refused to read the *News*. She sat in front of the camera, in the Angela Rippon chair, with her feet on the desk in a most un-Angela Rippon-like manner. "Read the *News*," said other members of the group, off-screen, but on the soundtrack. "I don't want to read the *News*." "Oh, go on. Read the *News*." "There's no *News* to read." "If we give you some *News*, will you read it?" Somebody handed the girl some news. "You call that *News*?" she said with contempt.

Nobody needed to explain to this group that the *News* is manufactured. They demonstrated their awareness of that by imagining a newsreader without news.

Another exercise, however, demonstrated that the *News* was normally manufactured from a particular point of view. First, we examined a lengthy interview with Arthur Scargill, the left-wing trade union leader. We tried to learn what we could about both his language and the way he sees society. Next we recorded a half-hour *News* programme from television – we used the *News* programme that happened to be on during the lunch-hour of that particular day: there were items on power strikes, a film report on South Africa's coal industry, some news from Rhodesia. Then we imagined that the *script* of the *News* had been written by Arthur Scargill instead of by some BBC news editor. What changes would Scargill have made in the *way* those particular items was reported? Finally, we wrote a new Scargill script to accompany the visuals of the *News* programme we'd been studying, and recorded the new script on the soundtrack of the BBC *News*, so that we had a finished tape of BBC visuals accompanied by our own Arthur Scargill soundtrack (spoken by a "newsreader" from the group) in which workers didn't "threaten" to strike but "promised" to do so.

A similar game with the *News* was played the other way round, when we recorded a *News* programme, kept the original soundtrack, but replaced all the filmed visuals by a variety of picture postcards and other stills, thrown in at random to accompany the script. The newsreader could be talking about "terrorist" activities in Northern Ireland – while on the monitor there would be holiday postcards. This game produced moments of very funny video: but it also helped to confirm how unnecessary much of the visual accompaniment to a typical TV *News* programme really is.

Playing with the medium sometimes led to technical discoveries. One group, for example, discovered how to make collective cartoons.

A camera is fixed facing a blank sheet of paper on the wall. One person puts a mark on the piece of paper. The camera is then switched on, and the mark is recorded for about twenty seconds. The camera is switched off, and the videotape re-wound for ten seconds. A second person adds a second mark. This is then recorded for twenty seconds, and the videotape is re-wound for another ten seconds. The process is repeated until everybody in the group has added to the drawing and until the group are satisfied that the picture is finished. When the tape is played back, the effect is that viewers first see a blank screen. Then a mark appears on the screen as if by magic. After ten seconds another mark appears. Then after another ten seconds, a third mark. Viewers see the cartoon being built up in front of their eyes.

The group who made a drawing of their own school and then set fire to it was using this method.

The "mixed ability media studies" course described in *The Times Educational Supplement* works on the assumption that pupils need to "study" the media in order to "evaluate". We found that pupils were more familiar with the language of some programmes than we were ourselves. The group who did a highly irreverent and

scurrilous version of *This Is Your Life* had clearly already
"evaluated" the programme – which was why they handled
it in the way they did.

In the same way a group of unemployed West Indians we
worked with in Bradford, who had formed themselves into a
Reggae band, had no need to make a "close study" of *Top
of the Pops* to discover how mindless and vapid the
programme was. They'd already rejected it in favour of
making their own music.

Rather than examining the negative qualities of
programmes that were not worth examining, we
concentrated on ways of using television language positively.
How could the cheek of Ronnie Barker in the prison
situation of *Porridge* be used by young people to cope with
their own school situation? What could a group of young
West Indians making a gangster film in Bradford learn from
their knowledge of *The Sweeney*?

It was this emphasis on what was positive and useful in
popular television language that led to the most complex
example of how existing television may be taken and
changed so that it becomes part of a new experience.

The example comes, not from the Bradford project, but
from a project which brought drama students and footballers
in Melbourne together in the making of a multi-media show
specifically for the supporters of Collingwood Football Club.
The entertainment we invented was called *The Grand Grand
Final Show*, and it was built around the videotape of one of
the most sensational Grand Finals every played in the
Victorian Football League – the match between Collingwood
and North Melbourne in 1977.

Roberta Bonnin (my Australian colleague who had worked
on the Bradford project) had acquired the videotape of the
1977 Grand Final from one of the commercial TV channels
in Melbourne, Channel 7. She, Ray Mooney (a Melbourne
playwright, who is also physical education instructor at
Collingwood Football Club) and I had dreamt up the project

as a celebration of Australian Rules Football. Channel 7 is the channel which provides the main coverage in Melbourne of Victorian Football League matches. From the first, therefore, we were directly involved in popular entertainment television.

To understand the significance of the project, it's necessary to know something of the part the Victorian Football League (VFL) plays in Melbourne life. Melbourne is the one city in the world where Australian Rules Football is played at first class levels and so football has become Melbourne's unique contribution to popular culture. During the season (which runs from April to September) nearly a tenth of the city's population attends the six VFL matches every Saturday. On Grand Final day in September, more than 100,000 spectators pack the Melbourne Cricket Ground, while virtually the entire population of the city watches the game live on Channel 7. In 1976, a political battle in Collingwood's boardroom gave Australian playwright David Williamson material for his internationally successful play, *The Club*. At the beginning of 1980, the dismissal of Carlton club's President, and the resignation of the club's player-coach were enough to keep the Soviet invasion of Afghanistan in second place on the Melbourne papers' front page. Victorian League Football has frequently been described as Melbourne's religion.

Collingwood is one of the oldest clubs in the VFL. The club has won more championship pennants than any other club in the League. But, to the frustration of the club's fanatical supporters, Collingwood has won nothing since 1958. Nearly every season, the club ends amongst the top five (who play off against each other in a series of matches known as the Finals): and frequently Collingwood reaches the Grand Final itself, only to fail at the last hurdle. The Grand Final has by now become something of a psychological nightmare to players and supporters. Rival supporters taunt Collingwood with banners: "Collingwood are like the snow – they melt in September".

The 1977 Grand Final – the videotape of which we used in our *Grand Grand Final Show* – was particularly traumatic for Collingwood. The previous year, Collingwood had ended bottom of the ladder, and it was this catastrophe that had provoked the upheaval presented in David Williamson's play. Collingwood had previously prided itself on being a "family" club: the coach (the equivalent of a soccer manager) had always been appointed from amongst the club's former players. The upheaval led to the appointment of a highly successful outside coach, Tommy Hafey: but there was a good deal of opposition to his appointment from the club's more conservative members. His first season with Collingwood, therefore, was being watched with more than usual interest.

What added spice to the 1977 Grand Final was that Hafey's personal rival, the most famous coach in the VFL, Ron Barassi, was in charge of the team Collingwood were playing against – North Melbourne. Hafey is a quiet, thoughtful, non-dramatic person: Barassi is in every way his opposite – verbal, flamboyant, a kind of successful Malcolm Allison. Collingwood are known as the Magpies. Barassi was later reported to have exhorted his players by screaming: "I want fried magpie for my supper. And fried magpie goes very well with champagne."

Hafey had achieved a great deal by lifting Collingwood from the foot of the ladder the previous season and taking them into the Grand Final: but the question on the lips of the entire population of Melbourne was whether or not he could break the hoodoo that had seemed to be on the club in the Grand Final for nineteen years.

Scoring is very high in Australian Rules Football: a goal counts as six points, and a near miss (a "behind") counts as one. Draws are very rare.

The game is played in four quarters of roughly twenty-five minutes each: and at the beginning of the final quarter of the 1977 Grand Final, Collingwood were winning by 28 points. (It was as if an English soccer team were winning 3 − 0 in the Wembley Cup Final with only half-an-hour to go.) Inspired, so it was later said, by Barassi, North Melbourne gradually whittled away the lead. With only a few minutes to go, North Melbourne were six points ahead. In the last minutes, Collingwood scored a goal to equalise, and the Grand Final ended in a draw. Collingwood lost the replay easily the following week.

It's difficult for people who don't live in Melbourne and haven't encountered Collingwood supporters to savour the drama of that last quarter. But almost every incident of the quarter is engraved in Collingwood memories − so that when we decided to use the videotape as the climax of our show, we were using a piece of television that was already part of the audience's vocabulary. And so we were free to play with the tape as the school-leavers in Bradford had played with the videotape of the news: only this time we were re-arranging material that was of real importance to the viewers.

Once we'd familiarised ourselves with the tape, we invited the Collingwood players to our studio. We set the situation very carefully. Taking tinnies − cans of beer − to the footy is part of the Melbourne ritual. And so we sat down with the players in front of the monitor, as if we were all spectators at a game, and we all drank tinnies and watched. But we turned off Channel 7's recorded commentary, so that the players were free to comment themselves on what they were seeing.

At first the atmosphere was jokey, with the players mocking each other's mistakes and cheering ironically if anybody did anything right. But as the drama mounted and the tape rolled relentlessly on, the players themselves became increasingly grabbed by the tension. "It always hurts me to watch this," said the club captain, Ray Shaw. When a player missed an easy goal near the end, there were groans: "If he'd scored that we'd have won." It was as if everybody was desperately trying to change the bit of history frozen on the tape. When Collingwood equalised towards the end, there was an immense collective sigh of relief, even though everyone had known the equaliser was coming.

Immediately after the tape was finished, we invited those players who had been in the 1977 Grand Final to sit in front of our video cameras and record, together, their comments on what they had just seen. Because they were still involved by the actual drama, their comments were completely different from those of professional footballers who are interviewed in programmes like *Match of the Day*. Footballers on TV programmes are in the hands of the TV "experts". In this videotape, the players were themselves in control – and so they talked without feeling the need to project a public image. They became skilled craftsmen talking to each other in their own language about their own craft. And when one of them said, "Seeing this tape will make us try harder in the future", one of the oldest members of the team commented ruthlessly, "We studied it before the replay, but it didn't make us try harder then."

The videotape we recorded contains what must be a unique picture of footballers talking about the game analytically, while still experiencing the aftermath of emotions aroused by having watched what had been for them a disastrous half-hour's football. And immediately after making this recording, three of the biggest names in Australian Rules football went on to record an improvised assault on the way the media usually treat them.

Every Thursday throughout the season, Channel 7 features a late-night chat programme called *League Teams*. Three regular football critics – usually veteran players – go through the teams that have been announced that night for all the following Saturday's matches, analysing the form of every individual player.

The critics are known as "the Three Wise Men", and the format is very loose. Drinks flow along with the chat, and the Three Wise Men have, over the years, come to be regarded as comedians as well as being football experts. The programme is watched by many people as much for the improvised comedy as for the information about football.

The players, however, see the programme differently.

Often, the Channel 7 experts have the names of the players selected before the players themselves have been told – and so the younger players, particularly those who are on the edge of the team and waiting to be selected for the first time, sit staring at the set, waiting to hear their names announced. Since the programme is open-ended, and the chat often goes on for hours, the players naturally find the programme frustrating. And they resent being analysed by people who have either never played the game at all, or who haven't played it for years.

Still raging from having failed to win the 1977 Grand Final, three of the senior players, Ray Shaw, René Kink and Peter Moore (their names would be as well-known in Victoria as the name of Kevin Keegan in Europe), sat down in front of our video camera and set up their own version of *League Teams*. Instead of the whisky in elegant glasses, they stuck cans of beer on the table. One of the "experts" regularly gives a recipe for a meal during the TV programme, so René Kink got potato crisps and peanuts and poured beer over them and began to mix up the mess on the table.

Ray Shaw wrote out a list of football critics on the back of an envelope, and the three of them went down the list, analysing the critics. "Well, he might be O.K. for tennis, but he doesn't know much about football. He once criticised my performance in a game when I wasn't even playing." "If you don't play for Geelong, so-and-so doesn't recognise your existence." "They never come round normally, but if there's a sniff of trouble in the club they all come to watch training." Ray Shaw picked up a knife and pretended to stick it in his own back. "Guess who," he said, and they all named the same critic. Peter Moore summed up the players' feelings when he said, "It's all right for them making jokes and talking about recipes, but it's our life. When I was a young kid hoping to get into the team, I used to sit there for hours watching them, and then they announced the actual names so quickly that I'd sometimes miss them. 'Mother: am I in the team ...?' " "What do they *really* know about what it's like to play football?" another player asked. "Well," came the answer, "there's always Jack Dyer. Captain Blood." (Dyer's one of the experts who was himself a star many years ago.) "Jack Dyer?" said the first player. "Is he still alive?"

Australian Rules Football players are popularly supposed to be big, dumb, beer-drinking thugs. These three players satirised their own image, by covering the table with beer cans and potato crisps, but they proved themselves highly articulate and quick-witted. Drama students watching them commented that the players were better at improvising than they themselves were. Afterwards, the players wanted to make the tape again, because they remembered points they'd left out – but the original version had a freshness, and they agreed to let it stand.

The evening's recording worked because players and students and all of us were involved in a dramatic context. The importance of such a context was demonstrated when, a few evenings later, we went with a video portapak to a training session and were introduced to the club's backroom boys. We tried to get them talking as freely as the players had talked – but because the dramatic context was missing, they simply responded to us as they would respond to professional TV interviewers, and all we got was official reality: Collingwood was a great club, Tommy Hafey was a great coach, the players were great ... After the camera was switched off, one of them said, "Now we'll tell you what we really think ...", but he wouldn't go on talking in front of the camera.

As well as working with the players on video, we made sound-recordings of the coach, Tommy Hafey, and of a number of supporters. The supporters were keen enough to be present at a pre-season training session. Once again their involvement in the context and their commitment to the game itself made them talk freely. Some of the older supporters described incidents in Grand Finals decades ago.

Tommy Hafey talked into the tape recorder for several hours, describing, as a professional who had spent much of his life thinking about the game, his ideas and his approach. He saw the show we were preparing as an opportunity to communicate his thinking to supporters — so he, too, was talking in a particular context.

Having gathered this material, we took the original 1977 Grand Final videotape and worked on it. We prepared a version which opened with the original sound commentary. Then, after a few minutes, we cut on to the soundtrack extracts from the tape Tommy Hafey had made: the extracts were carefully chosen so that general comments were being made about specific incidents in the game. (For example, Hafey would be talking about the way he drills players, in defensive situations, to pick up and follow opposing players, while on the screen would be shown an incident in which his players failed to do this and left an opposing player free.) Then we cut on the soundtrack from Hafey, the modern expert, to old supporters talking about previous Grand Finals, while the 1977 Grand Final went on unrolling on the screen. At critical moments we faded in again the original commentary. As the final quarter drew towards its climax, we cut in the video recording of the players talking about their own performance, returning to the original videotape for the final equalising goal. And then, as the videotape showed the exhausted players walking off the field, Tommy Hafey's voice was heard on the soundtrack, talking about his hopes for the 1979 season.

When we showed this version of the 1977 Grand Final, together with the players' own version of *League Teams*, as the climax of our entertainment, to the supporters at the Collingwood Social Club, we were using the familiar language of popular television for an unfamiliar dramatic purpose. The audience was already familiar with the original tape. But the comments of Hafey, the old supporters and the players themselves put the tape into a new light. The supporters were put into a different relationship with the players and with Hafey. A shot of a familiar player doing what was familiar on the screen — catching and kicking a football — was immediately followed by an unfamiliar shot of the same player, talking with his colleagues, or performing as a critic on the screen. Moreover, the fact that the players were there, watching the new version of the tape, alongside the supporters, gave the whole evening an added dimension. The videotape became part of the collective experience of supporters and players alike.

The show drew on other elements of popular language. For example, a book had been published in Melbourne about the experiences of the rival North Melbourne coach, Ron Barassi, during the 1977 season. It quoted, allegedly, word for word what Barassi had said to his players during the Grand Final against Collingwood. We made a piece of video in which the master of ceremonies for the evening, a student called Ross Williams, harangued the rest of the actors, supposedly in their dressing-room, about their performances during the opening half of the show: "We rehearsed those lines again and again," Ross screamed at a girl who was being treated for an "injury", "and when you got out there in front of the audience, you forgot your lines. You forgot your bloody lines. *Why did you forget your bloody lines?*" ... The audience recognised, in delight, a reference to Barassi screaming at the North Melbourne players that they'd forgotten what he'd told them. And, suddenly, a surprising new connection was drawn between footballers and actors.

Again, for many years, there had been at Collingwood a star player, Phil Carman, who always wore white boots. In a controversial move, Hafey had sacked him at the end of the 1978 season. Carman wrote for a popular Melbourne paper, *The Observer*, and only the week before we put on our show, he'd accused Hafey in his column of not understanding stars. In our show, we had an actor with white boots, who was also sacked. When he was sacked, he accused the master of ceremonies of not understanding stars.

The audience immediately recognised the reference, and responded warmly to Hafey, who was there in the room.

The *Grand Grand Final Show* offers an example of how it's possible to take the language of popular television, popular sport and popular journalism and put it together in such a way as to offer people a new dramatic experience. The experience clearly entertained the audience. But it also taught all of us a great deal. It taught drama students about football, and, therefore, about an important element in Melbourne popular culture. It taught footballers about drama, and about the possibilities of theatre, and about how they might use television for their own purposes rather than for the purposes of the TV "experts". It taught the audience to look at both football and theatre in a different way. And it taught everybody about the history of the Victorian Football League, and, therefore, about the social history of Melbourne.

Most important of all, though, from my point of view, was the model of one possible form of popular education which the project created. It was a model based on popular wants.

Those of us who made the show didn't make it because, as "teachers" or "artists" we felt that we *ought* to make "community theatre". We made it because we were Australian Rules Football enthusiasts. (One girl who joined the project for personal reasons certainly became an enthusiast as the work evolved.) Most of us were Collingwood supporters. We wanted to do something for and with the Club. We were delighted to meet and work with the players and to learn from them. We wanted to celebrate our own enjoyment of the game. The language of popular entertainment was our language too. We came together in the project with other people who shared our wants.

It is out of an extension of people's wants that any genuinely popular forms of education are going to be developed.

At the beginning of the 1980's, the need to develop such forms is becoming increasingly clear. After one hundred years of compulsory education, the system we've got is demonstrably failing to achieve its declared aim of offering equality of opportunity and greater social mobility. The percentage of the school population going on to higher education has actually *fallen* from 16% in the early 1970's to an estimated 12% in the early 1980's. Three out of every four of the successful minority still come from middle-class backgrounds. According to A. H. Halsey (*Origins and Destinations*) it was as difficult for a working-class boy to get a Grammer School education in the 1950's as it had been seventy years earlier. So far there is no evidence that the introduction of the comprehensive system has made any impact on the traditional class patterns.

The education we've got was imposed on the majority by a paternalist elite. The intention was to "help" the majority to become mature, equal, participating members of a democratic society. But the effect was to put working-class children in the hands of a group of mainly middle-class teachers and give that group the right to impose its own values. Education has, therefore, been caught in its own contradictions.

One of the central contradictions is illustrated by the gap between what teachers would like to achieve, and what their position forces on them.

The teachers in Granada's *Open Day*, when asked why they became teachers, offered a number of idealistic reasons: "I wanted to spread the gospel of socialism"; "I wanted to do something that would be of value to other people in society"; "I was concerned about the state of the world".

But contrast these idealistic intentions with the description by a teacher in a Halifax Secondary Modern School of his position in January 1980.

"Your son should do well in the examination," he tells a parent. "I hope he does. He deserves to. He works hard. There's a clique in the class that doesn't work and that tries to stop other people from working. Some kids get distracted by them, but your son takes no notice. He just keeps on working."

"The trouble is," the teacher continues, "there are no sanctions nowadays. I could soon sort them out, but I'm not allowed to thump them. There's one boy in the class – he's a lot bigger than I am, over six foot. But his mother came to me and said, 'If ever he gives any trouble, belt him'. I know I'm all right with him. But there are some parents who'd be down here threatening me with the law. School-teaching's a good job. I could get black-listed and lose my job. And jobs are hard to come by these days.

"It'll be worse soon, when the Government's education cuts begin to take effect. I've got twenty in the class at the moment, but with fewer teachers, classes will get bigger again soon."

The teacher is clearly as conscientious and committed as the teachers in *Open Day*. He desperately wants his pupils to get on. He knows that they will only get on by passing examinations. So he concentrates on teaching the ambitious few how to pass examinations. He teaches History – so at some time he's presumably been interested in the subject. But the examiners demand that his pupils should be able to recognise a dot on the map where Wilberforce was born, so he spends his time teaching them to recognise and name Kingston-upon-Hull.

Not surprisingly, most of the pupils in the class, who don't expect to pass examinations anyway, don't see the point of being able to recognise and name the place where Wilberforce was born. They don't much care who Wilberforce was anyway – and learning how to recognise dots on maps is hardly likely to persuade them that they ought to care. So they pass the time as entertainingly as they can: but this, of course, disrupts the teacher and the pupils who *are* trying to "work".

In the interests of those who are trying to work, the teacher wishes he could sort the rest out by thumping them –

but the parents would object, and the law would be against him. He succeeds in implying that the law is somehow unreasonable: and from his point of view it is. It stops him from doing the job of "helping" his pupils.

Many thoroughly respectable people would agree with the teacher's attitude: after all, he's clearly a reasonable, commonsense man. Yet if, outside a classroom, a man threatened to sort out his problems by thumping people under his control, he'd be regarded as a potential violent criminal. This teacher isn't a violent criminal. The system he's caught in makes him think like one.

The education we've got is designed to develop civilised human beings. Yet its effect is to put a civilised man into a position where he feels the need to use violence.

The contradiction in which this particular teacher is caught reflects the central contradiction of the education industry. The education system we've got was created from above by people in a position of power. Their intentions, like this teacher's, were unquestionably good. At every stage – in the 1870's when compulsion was first introduced, in 1944 with the arrival of secondary education for all, and in the 1960's when the comprehensive system was extended – they belived that they were making Lowndes' "silent social revolution" possible.

But a revolution involves a transfer of power. A silent social revolution implies that those in power are willing to relinquish that power, voluntarily. The inventors of our education system never had any intention of doing that. They were certain, on the contrary, that they needed to have power so that they could use it on behalf of people less fortunate than themselves – just as the Halifax teacher believes that he needs the right to thump some pupils for the good of others.

The inventors of the system saw what they had created in terms of throwing out a life-line which would enable talented and lucky working-class children to climb out of their own class and join the people in power.

The result was that they built a structure in which working-class children could only be successful in middle-class terms.

While recognising that so far middle-class children have had all the benefits from compulsory education, A. H. Halsey argues that the system should be *extended*, because, he says, middle-class demand is now saturated so that further investment can only benefit the bright working-class child.

Similarly, the *Guardian*'s education correspondent, Maureen O'Conner, argues that, if the present system of compulsory education were abolished, middle-class children would benefit because middle-class families would know how to make better use of whatever non-compulsory system took its place. The implication is that it's impossible to imagine an education system in which working-class children could have an advantage.

Both Halsey's and Maureen O'Conner's arguments ignore another possible explanation of the failure of the educationalists to provide equality of opportunity: and that is that the system has built-in elements which ensure that middle-class children are more likely to succeed, and that these elements have been built in precisely for that purpose.

Consider, for example, the way literacy is measured in our education system.

Literacy is important in so far as it can help us win some control over our own lives. Before the introduction of compulsory education, literacy was struggled for by working men and women who formed Reading Societies. The struggle was part of a more general political struggle. The children of Female Reformers in Blackburn learnt a "Bad Alphabet": B was for Bible, Bishop and Bigotry; K was for King, King's Evil, Knave and Kidnappers; W was for Whig, Weakness, Wavering and Wicked.

In our own century, in rural Brazil, Paulo Freire, working alongside non-literate peasants, has struggled to develop ways of learning to read and write that are rooted in the peasants' working experience. Freire writes:

> I can see validity only in a literacy program in which men
> understand words in their true significance: as a force to
> transform the world. As illiterate men discover the relativity
> of ignorance and of wisdom, they destroy one of the myths
> by which false elites have manipulated them.

In our education industry, the way people are taught to think
of language itself involves manipulation by an elite. People's
commonsense belief in the value of literacy has been
changed into a blind faith that literacy is effectively measured
by an examination, invented and then marked by the elite.
Access to higher education and to a wide range of jobs has
been made dependent on success in this examination (GCE
O level English Language).

The form of this examination reflects the elite's
assumptions about what constitutes literacy. Pupils are
required to write to order for a given length of time on one of
a number of given topics (a skill, incidentally, never
normally required outside an examination room). The topics
themselves tell us what the examiners think a literate person
ought to be interested in:

> "Do you consider that we live in a violent age?"
> "The Art of Choosing and Wearing Clothes"
> " 'Towns, with their ring-roads and subways and concrete
> centres, are changing for the worse.' Do you support this
> view?"
> " 'God gave us our relatives; thank goodness we can
> choose our friends.' Do you agree with this view?"

They're the kind of topics that would be discussed,
genteelly, for and against, in the homes of comfortable
professional families over coffee after Sunday lunch. And the
very phrasing of the questions invites working-class pupils to
try and write in a language that isn't their own: (working-
class kids might well talk about how much they spend on

clothes and why they buy what they do, but they'd never, unless they were talking ironically, refer to the "Art" of choosing and wearing clothes). The kind of young people the examiners have in mind when they set the topics is implied in another question involving a long quotation from Maurice Wiggin:

> "Mine was a happy childhood. A sense of family unity; loving and indulgent parents who nevertheless had high principles; a modest affluence; a comfortable home; great companionship allied with a taste for solitude and adventures – these were the ingredients." Which aspects of your childhood are you sorry to have left behind, and which make you feel glad that you are older now?

To West Indian adolescents living in inner city high-rise flats, (the kind described by a Liverpool policeman on television as "a dustbin"), or to the children of one-parent mothers on decaying council house estates, the world described by Maurice Wiggin is a foreign land. And the language of that land is a foreign language. Compare Wiggin's language with that of, Sheila, a Bradford woman describing the house she lives in.

> I've been up here for over four years now and I haven't had anything done, no repairs or anything. I've loose floorboards, all my staircase is damp, it's black with damp. We spent £14 on painting that when we first come up here; you're supposed to keep decently decorated, but you can't do that with that staircase of mine, because as fast as you do that – you see, there's no air in ... They've been promising to re-wire ever since I moved up here. There are no points upstairs. They said when they took the gasfires out they would put points in for some kind of heating, but heat, there is none upstairs. ... So you can well imagine how damp it is in winter. They came and put a sink unit and they sent a fellow to plaster afterwards, and he fractured a gas-pipe on the cooker, and he said, "I'll come back and do it", and it's still waiting to be done.

Sheila was talking into a tape-recorder. Unlike the language of the examination papers, her language is simple, clear, matter-of-fact, urgent. But confronted with a question like: "Discuss the arguments in favour of holidays abroad as compared with holidays in your own country, and state your preferences", she wouldn't know where to begin. The way the question is stated is alien. Asked, "Would you rather go to Blackpool or Majorca?", she'd probably say, "Who's paying the fare?" A Maurice Wiggin would probably begin: "In considering the question of whether holidays abroad are preferable to holidays at home, a number of factors must be taken into consideration ..."

The *form* of an examination, the results of which are used to limit possibilities open to those who fail, ensures that the Maurice Wiggins are much more likely to succeed than the Sheilas.

Sheila talks naturally all the time of "they". She's come to accept that "they" will dictate the conditions of her life. The first "they" that working-class children encounter are teachers: the lesson that "they" are in total control is learnt early. The only way to get on, pupils learn, is to become one of "them", learn "their" language.

Literacy is measured in terms which make it far easier for middle-class children to succeed than for working-class children. And, since teaching right across the board is done in "their" language, this affects the chances of working-class children in almost every aspect of education.

From the point of view of the people being educated, power in the education system is totally in the hands of "them". "They" decide when children must go to school. "They" have put the schools where they are. "They" group children into classes at "their" convenience. "They" decide what shall be taught and when, decreeing a limited number of subjects to be academically respectable. "They" appoint people to teach these subjects – pupils can't choose their own teachers as an adult might choose a driving instructor. The teachers, like the system, are imposed by "them" and are given almost unlimited power to pass judgement on the pupils.

Pupils are judged – rewarded and punished, "passed" or "failed" – entirely on terms invented by "them". Moreover, as the power of the education industry has grown over the century, "their" claims to be able to measure a pupil's capabilities have been increasingly accepted by people in power outside the industry, such as employers. The more rewarding jobs are increasingly reserved for those who have been licensed by the education industry, who have been given certificates, diplomas and degrees.

Far from increasing social mobility and equality of opportunity, the education industry is helping to ensure that there are *fewer* opportunities for the bright working-class pupil who didn't do well at school and who, therefore, has no paper qualifications. The "they" who award the certificates claim the right to dictate what a child's future will be. If the pupil can't fulfil "their" expectations, then the pupil's own expectations must be dramatically limited.

Given this situation, it is scarcely surprising that the great majority of the population – and particularly of working-class school-leavers – is alienated from education in all its authority-organised forms.

And yet, a great many of us still believe that education *can* be used to enable people to learn to control their own lives. If education can't radically change society, it can at least offer experiences which make radical change conceivable.

If education is to be used for change, though, education itself has got to be changed. And change involves the creation of new forms: which is what the work described in this book is about.

Nobody would argue that a few video projects offer a satisfactory way out of our educational and social dilemmas. But, given the present situation, it seems to me urgent for those of us who do believe in change to work positively to create as many working models of change as possible. The video projects represented one attempt to create working models.

Alongside the video projects we were developing other models. One was built round the production of a weekly news-sheet by unemployed people. The paper called *Happy Days (Are Here Again)* was written, and distributed in the dole queues, by a group of unemployed, and led to other activities, including the formation of a *Don't be Doleful on the Dole* band, which played in the dole office until it was expelled by the police. Another model was based on work done with a group of women and children on a Bradford council house estate, which has been described as "the Third World of Bradford". The women produced their monthly paper, learning to use tape-recorders to get contributions: people simply talked into the sound-recorder, and what they said was transcribed and published. Other women began by using cameras to take photos of their own children on an outing – and went on to collect pictures of broken doors, boarded-up windows and other evidence of council neglect. (This work brought us into a head-on clash with the housing authorities when the unemployed mother of five who was typing the paper was threatened with eviction because of a bureaucratic error.)

Elsewhere, groups of unemployed young people found places to survive by entertaining each other with music. In Liverpool, on the site of the Cavern Club where the Beatles once played, a venue called Brady's (formerly Eric's) Club has become the centre of small local groups who play to young people at £50 a gig, and cut the odd single on a local label which is linked with the club. The aim isn't openly "educational", but, as one of the young men who runs it – who himself left school at 16 and later worked as a binman – put it, the club exists for creative kids of all kinds to find a platform to develop their talents. Brady's Club survives commercially at prices young people on the dole can afford. If a network of such venues could develop, and if other activities besides the making of popular music could be accommodated, it would be possible to see such places beginning to form yet another framework for popular education.

The particular contribution made by the video projects seems to me to lie in the use we made of the language of popular television *entertainment*. The stress on "entertainment" is important. Television news, information and education services use "their" language, the language of authority. It's in the interests of authority to mystify – hence the fact that issues such as unemployment are naturally described in language that's alien to unemployed people.

The language of such programmes as *The Morecambe and Wise Show*, *The Sweeney*, *The Two Ronnies*, *Porridge*, *The Last of the Summer Wine*, *Oh, No! It's Selwyn Froggitt*, and of many more popular programmes, is sceptical, irreverent, down-to-earth, de-mystifying. Not simply the verbal language, the way words are used – in *The Last of the Summer Wine*, for example, three old men living in a Yorkshire village use highly literary forms of expression to highly comic effect. It's the whole language of such programmes (their way of looking and communicating, the attitudes they express) that gives them their perkiness and bounce.

In our video work we tried to take that bounce and push it further, until the implicitly irreverent and sceptical language could be used consciously to question existing social arrangements.

Such questioning seems to me an essential first step towards changing these social arrangements. The language in which the questions can be asked needs to be a language that belongs to the people who are doing the asking.

The television entertainers have helped to forge a language. The video work explored ways of using it.

APPENDIX

by Ken Sparne

The results of working with video and alternative television depend more on attitude and methodology, than on the sophistication of the available technology. A number of schools throughout the country as well as most colleges of higher and further education and all universities have some form of television system. These are variously described as television centres, educational technology, audio-visual aids, library and learning resource, closed-circuit television, etc. They generally assume that what broadcast television does and how is the be-all and end-all in standards of perfection, both in terms of content and technical quality. There is rarely if ever, therefore, a conscious effort to break away from imitating the established conventions of broadcast television.

On the other hand there is an increasing number of video workshops throughout the country with a much more open and innovative approach. Within formal education a similar approach is more likely to be found in adult education, community education centres and various types of outreach educational work. A useful guide to nearly ninety such projects can be found in:

Animation Projects in the U.K.
Printed and published by the National Youth Bureau, from whom copies are available. Price: £1.50.
National Youth Bureau, 17/23 Albion Street, Leicester LE1 6GD.

For more detailed and technical information on video a number of useful publications are available:

Video Distribution Handbook
Centre for Advanced TV Studies, Fantasy Factory, 42 Theobalds Road, London WC1. 1978. 56pp. ISBN 0 903795 03 5. £1.50 post free.

Includes a useful introduction to the technicalities of playing back videotapes, as well as listing a large number of videotapes, tape makers, distributors and sources of equipment in England and Wales, arranged according to regions.

Basic Video in Community Work
Inter-Action Advisory Service Handbook No. 5. Inter-Action Imprint, 15 Wilkin Street, London NW5. 1975. 32pp. ISBN 0 904571 05 X. Price: 75p.

Covers the use of video as a community development tool, running a video project, costs and funding, as well as how the equipment works and how to use it. Revised version, 1979.

VTR Workshop
By Loretta J. Atienza. UESCO, 7 Place de Fontenoy, 75700 Paris, France. 1977. 114pp. ISBN 92 3 101467 6. Available from Fantasy Factory, 42 Theobalds Road, London WC1. £1.80.

Written for use in developing countries, covers operating details, connections, editing, maintenance. Could be very useful to beginners in the U.K.

For information on a much wider range of alternative communications refer to:

COM COM
Community Communications Group, Information Officer, Derek Jones, 8 Millfield Close, Farndon, Cheshire.
Telephone: Home 0829 270554, Work 0925 51144 ext 150.

Directory of Video Tapes
Published and compiled by:
The London Community Video Workers Collective, c/o Walworth and Aylesbury Community Arts Trust, Shop 8, Taplow, East Street, Aylesbury Estate, London SE17.
Price: 25p, post free, to individuals and community groups; £2 to libraries, institutions and anyone who can afford it.

Details of the video equipment referred to in this book:

Sony Manufacture:

AV3620CE	Video Tape Recorder
AV3670ACE	Video Tape Recorder
AV3420CE	Portable Video Recorder
AVC3250CES	Camera
AVC3450CE	Portable Camera with zoom lens, viewfinder and built-in microphone
PVM90CE	Monochrome Monitor, without sound
PVM201CE	Monochrome Monitor, playback monitor
CMS110CE	Camera switcher fader
CMW110CE	Camera wiper effects unit
CG3CE	Sync pulse generator